Mastering SoapUI

Master the art of testing and automating your SOA
using SoapUI

Pranai Nandan

BIRMINGHAM - MUMBAI

Mastering SoapUI

First published: August 2016

Production reference: 1260816

Published by Packt Publishing Ltd.
Livery Place
35 Livery Street
Birmingham B3 2PB, UK.

ISBN 978-1-78398-080-2

www.packtpub.com

Credits

Author
Pranai Nandan

Reviewer
Dennis Knol

Acquisition Editor
Prachi Bisht

Content Development Editor
Trusha Shriyan

Technical Editor
Nirant Carvalho

Copy Editors
Safis Editing
Madhusudan Uchil

Project Coordinator
Kinjal Bari

Proofreader
Safis Editing

Indexer
Pratik Shirodkar

Graphics
Kirk D'Penha

Production Coordinator
Shantanu N. Zagade

Cover Work
Shantanu N. Zagade

About the Author

Pranai Nandan is a "Tester by Choice and Developer by birth" born in the small city of U.P Bareilly India he has come a long way in his life, he started his journey of his studies with Hartman college and temporarily ended it with a BTECH in Computer Science from Invertis university. Over the course of his professional careers he has worked in several geographies across the world including UK and Europe with different companies like QA Infotech, Hitachi Consulting, TIBCO Software's. Currently he works with Cognizant as a Senior Associate in Amsterdam Netherlands. His work in the Testing field has resulted in multiple Test Automation frameworks for different vertical including Retail, Telecom, Media and BFSI. Pranai Nandan is someone who is intrigued by test automation and implementing complex solutions for enterprise business applications to help them achieve their desired ROI.

Apart from SoapUI he also has expertise on other SOA test Automation and Virtualization tools including Ready API, IBM RIT, ITKO LISA, HP Service Virtualization. His technical expertise also includes tools like Selenium web driver, JMeter, Microsoft, VSTS, HP Load Runner and Jenkins.

His hobbies are writing poems, playing cricket, knowing about history of different culture& travelling.

Acknowledgments

I have been helped by several people in my life and those learnings and experiences have made me what I am today I would first like to thank my Mother "Kusum Lata" who herself is the biggest source of inspiration to me she is someone who has loved me the most and laid down the principles of values and rite in me. A big thanks to my father, most gentle man I have ever known "Devki Nandan" for his wonderful guidance and support in my life.

I would also like to thank my two beautiful elder sisters who have loved me taught me the meaning of right and wrong "Preeti Srivastava" & "Jyoti Srivastava" and last but not the least I would like to thank my would be wife and my friend from a long time "Sneha Singh" who has been the best of friend to me for long time she is someone who has motivated me on my rough days and celebrated my victorious moments.

Winners Don't Do different Things they Do Things Differently

About the Reviewer

Dennis Knol has worked for more than 10 years as a test engineer at various companies and on various projects. Due to his background as a developer, he started with automated testing. As it became more fun and interesting, he decided to continue with it. Over the course of several years, he has gathered a lot of experience with a broad selection of tools, such as Selenium, Rational Robot, HP Quick Test Pro, and TTWorkbench, and worked with several programming languages, such as Java, .NET, Visual Basic, and TTCN-3.

www.PacktPub.com

eBooks, discount offers, and more

Did you know that Packt offers eBook versions of every book published, with PDF and ePub files available? You can upgrade to the eBook version at www.PacktPub. com and as a print book customer, you are entitled to a discount on the eBook copy. Get in touch with us at customercare@packtpub.com for more details.

At www.PacktPub.com, you can also read a collection of free technical articles, sign up for a range of free newsletters and receive exclusive discounts and offers on Packt books and eBooks.

https://www2.packtpub.com/books/subscription/packtlib

Do you need instant solutions to your IT questions? PacktLib is Packt's online digital book library. Here, you can search, access, and read Packt's entire library of books.

Why subscribe?

- Fully searchable across every book published by Packt
- Copy and paste, print, and bookmark content
- On demand and accessible via a web browser

Table of Contents

Preface

Mastering SoapUI as the name suggests is book which is all about Soap UI. The book provides the in-depth knowledge of functional, security, and performance testing on service-oriented architecture by using SoapUI. This book also explains you industry standard test automation framework based on SoapUI which are capable of invoking UI, database, and Web services. Through this book, readers would also come to know how we can leverage SoapUI for functional test automation and would learn to integrate SoapUI with tools like Jenkins, HP QC, and Selenium. We will also learn to create various reusable utilities for test automation. This book provides it readers with real time examples.

What this book covers

Chapter 1, Introduction to SOA Testing, introduces you to the key features of SoapUI, and by the end of this chapter, the readers will be familiar with SOA and SOA Testing. They will have a basic understanding of functional, load, and security testing in SOA using SoapUI.

Chapter 2, Functional Testing in Detail, explains the readers how to functionally test a web service using SoapUI. By the end of the chapter, they will be able to test web services and service orchestration functionality and will also know how to use the features such as XPath, Assertions, HermesJMS.

Chapter 3, Performance Testing of SOA Applications in Detail, discusses about performance testing of SOA using SoapUI and various load patterns. In this chapter, we would also see the integration of SoapUI with LoadUI.

Chapter 4, Security Testing in Detail, In this chapter, we will learn to configure security tests and validate the results .We will see how to configure the test types and add additional test criteria for each scan type using SoapUI.

Chapter 5, Test Automation in SOA World, will discuss test automation in detail and teach to create test automation frameworks and reusable assets for your automation framework, and designing an automation framework.

Chapter 6, Multilayer Test Automation Using SoapUI and Selenium, will teach Multilayer testing, Integration of selenium and SoapUI, Locator Identification for UI, and Automating Multilayers together using SoapUI and Selenium.

Chapter 7, SoapUI Integration with Jenkins and HP QC, will discuss about DevOps and the way we can achieve it by integrating SoapUI with Jenkins. You will also learn to integrate SoapUI with test management tools such as QC.

Chapter 8, End-to-End Test Automation, will explain how to create end-to-end test automation frameworks by integrating different tools and utilities together. This will provide a real-time view of end-to-end automation.

Chapter 9, Service Mocking, will discuss how to create mock services and deploy them. We will also learn to implement different dispatch type of the service as per our business needs.

Chapter 10, Best Practices in SOA Test Automation, will teach you about the best practices and guidelines for SOA test automation.

Chapter 11, Crack the Certification, can be found at `https://www.packtpub.com/sites/default/files/downloads/21130S_Chapter_11_Crack_the_Certification.pdf`.

What you need for this book

For this book, you would need the following software:

- SoapUI [O.S] 4.0 and higher
- Selenium Web driver Jars
- Jenkins
- JExcel Jar
- LoadUI
- Apache Ant 1.9.2

Who this book is for

The book is intended for test architects, SOA test specialists, automation testers, test managers, and software developers who have a good understanding of SOA, web services, Groovy Scripting, and the SoapUI tool.

Conventions

In this book, you will find a number of text styles that distinguish between different kinds of information. Here are some examples of these styles and an explanation of their meaning.

Code words in text, database table names, folder names, filenames, file extensions, pathnames, dummy URLs, user input, and Twitter handles are shown as follows: "We are storing the results to the database as an `ActualDomainHit` and we are comparing it against the expected values."

A block of code is set as follows:

```
def rows = sql.rows("select * from PROJECT where name like 'Pranai%'")
assert rows.size() == 2
```

Any command-line input or output is written as follows:

```
set Script=C:\\SOAP_Test\
  cd %Script%
 call ant -f  Build.xml
set Script=C:\\mfg
  %progdrive%
cd %Script%


 call ant -f Build.xml


pause(100000000000000)
```

New terms and **important words** are shown in bold. Words that you see on the screen, for example, in menus or dialog boxes, appear in the text like this: "Select the name of the security test and click on **OK**."

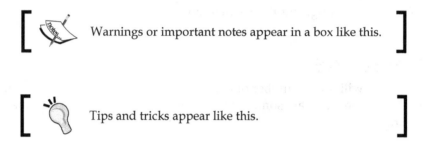

[Warnings or important notes appear in a box like this.]

[Tips and tricks appear like this.]

Reader feedback

Feedback from our readers is always welcome. Let us know what you think about this book—what you liked or disliked. Reader feedback is important for us as it helps us develop titles that you will really get the most out of.

To send us general feedback, simply e-mail feedback@packtpub.com, and mention the book's title in the subject of your message.

If there is a topic that you have expertise in and you are interested in either writing or contributing to a book, see our author guide at www.packtpub.com/authors.

Customer support

Now that you are the proud owner of a Packt book, we have a number of things to help you to get the most from your purchase.

Downloading the example code

You can download the example code files for this book from your account at http://www.packtpub.com. If you purchased this book elsewhere, you can visit http://www.packtpub.com/support and register to have the files e-mailed directly to you.

You can download the code files by following these steps:

1. Log in or register to our website using your e-mail address and password.
2. Hover the mouse pointer on the **SUPPORT** tab at the top.
3. Click on **Code Downloads & Errata**.
4. Enter the name of the book in the **Search** box.
5. Select the book for which you're looking to download the code files.
6. Choose from the drop-down menu where you purchased this book from.
7. Click on **Code Download**.

You can also download the code files by clicking on the **Code Files** button on the book's webpage at the Packt Publishing website. This page can be accessed by entering the book's name in the **Search** box. Please note that you need to be logged in to your Packt account.

Once the file is downloaded, please make sure that you unzip or extract the folder using the latest version of:

* WinRAR / 7-Zip for Windows
* Zipeg / iZip / UnRarX for Mac
* 7-Zip / PeaZip for Linux

The code bundle for the book is also hosted on GitHub at `https://github.com/PacktPublishing/Mastering-SoapUI`. We also have other code bundles from our rich catalog of books and videos available at `https://github.com/PacktPublishing/`. Check them out!

Errata

Although we have taken every care to ensure the accuracy of our content, mistakes do happen. If you find a mistake in one of our books — maybe a mistake in the text or the code — we would be grateful if you could report this to us. By doing so, you can save other readers from frustration and help us improve subsequent versions of this book. If you find any errata, please report them by visiting `http://www.packtpub.com/submit-errata`, selecting your book, clicking on the **Errata Submission Form** link, and entering the details of your errata. Once your errata are verified, your submission will be accepted and the errata will be uploaded to our website or added to any list of existing errata under the Errata section of that title.

To view the previously submitted errata, go to `https://www.packtpub.com/books/content/support` and enter the name of the book in the search field. The required information will appear under the **Errata** section.

Piracy

Piracy of copyrighted material on the Internet is an ongoing problem across all media. At Packt, we take the protection of our copyright and licenses very seriously. If you come across any illegal copies of our works in any form on the Internet, please provide us with the location address or website name immediately so that we can pursue a remedy.

Please contact us at `copyright@packtpub.com` with a link to the suspected pirated material.

We appreciate your help in protecting our authors and our ability to bring you valuable content.

Questions

If you have a problem with any aspect of this book, you can contact us at `questions@packtpub.com`, and we will do our best to address the problem.

Introduction to SOA Testing

With the increase in implementation of **service-oriented architecture (SOA)**, architecture across applications leads to various technological and business advantages to the organizations implementing it.

But as it's said; *There are two sides to every coin*, with SOA architecture came advantages such as the following:

- Reusability
- Better scalability
- Platform independency
- Business agility
- Enhanced security

But there are also disadvantages:

- Increased response time
- Service management effort is high
- Implementation cost is high

In this chapter we will study the following topics:

- Introduction to SOA
- SoapUI architecture
- Test levels in SOA testing
- SOA testing approach
- Introduction to functional, performance and security testing using SoapUI
- Is SOA really advantageous?

Well, let's talk about a few of the advantages of SOA architecture:

- **Reusability**: If we want to reuse the same piece of functionality exposed via a web service we should be absolutely sure that the functionality of the service is working as expected; security of the service is reliable and has no performance bottlenecks.

- **Business Agility**: With more functional changes being easily adopted in a web service, we make the web service prone to functional bugs.

- **Enhanced Security**: Web services are usually wrapped around systems that are being protected by several layers of security like SSL and usage of security tokens. Use of the business layer to protect the technical services to be directly exposed is usually handled by these layers. If the security of these layers is removed, the web service is highly vulnerable. Also the use of XML as a communication protocol opens the service to XML based attacks. So to mitigate risks we have **SOA** testing, and to help you test SOA architecture we have multiple testing tools on the market for example; SoapUI, SoapUI Pro, HP Service Test, ITKO LISA and SOA Parasoft.

But the most widely used and open source tool in the SOA testing arena is SoapUI. Following is a comparative analysis of the most famous tools in the Web service testing & test automation arena.

Comparative Analysis:

S.No	Factors	SoapUI	SaopUI PRO	ITKO LISA	SOA Parasoft
1	Cost	Open source	400 $/License	Highly Costly	Highly Costly
2	Multilayer testing	Yes	Yes	Yes	Yes
3	Scripting support	Yes	Yes	Yes	Yes
4	Protocol support	Yes	Yes	Yes	Yes
5	CI support	Yes	Yes	Yes	Yes
6	Ease of use	8/10	9/10	9/10	9/10
7	Learning curve	8/10	8/10	6/10	6/10

As we can see by the preceding comparison metrics, **Ease of use**, **Learning curve**, and **Cost** play a major role in selection of a tool for any project. So to learn **ITKO LISA** or **SOA Parasoft**, there is very limited, or no, material available on the Internet. To get resources trained you need to go to the owners of these tools and pay extra and then pay more if you need the training a second time.

This gives additional advantages to SoapUI and SoapUI Pro to be the first choice for Test Architects and Test Managers for their projects.

Now let's talk about the closely related brothers in this subset; SoapUI & SoapUI Pro are from the same family, Eviware, which is now SmartBear. However, SoapUI Pro has an enriched functionality and GUI which have additional functionalities to help reduce the time for testing, justifying its cost as compared to SoapUI open source.

Here is a quick comparison:

Criteria	SoapUI	SoapUI Pro
Reporting	Very limited, no rich reporting	Reports are available in different formats
XPath Builder	Not Available	Available
Data source	Not Available	Multiple options for data sources available
Data sink	Not Available	Available
XQuery Builder	Not Available	Available

The additional functionality that is available in SoapUI Pro can be achieved by SoapUI using Groovy script. To sum up everything that is given as UI functionality in SoapUI PRO is achievable with little effort in SoapUI which finally makes SoapUI open source the preferred choice for tool pickers.

SoapUI architecture

Before we move onto the architecture let's take a look the capabilities of SoapUI and how can we use it for the benefit of our projects.

SoapUI provides the following testing features to the test team:

- Functional testing [manual]
- Function test automation
- Performance testing
- Security testing
- Web service interoperability testing

Apart from these, SoapUI is also capable of integration with the following:

- LoadUI for advanced performance testing
- Selenium for multilayer testing
- Jenkins for continuous integration
- HP QC for end-to-end test automation management and execution

SoapUI has a comparatively simple architecture as compared to other tools in the SOA testing world.

The following image, shows the architecture of SoapUI at an overview level:

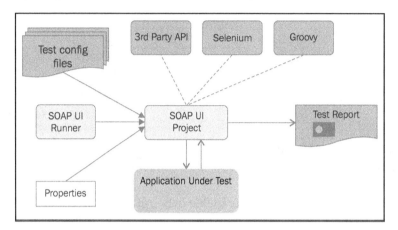

Let's talk about the architecture in detail:

- **Test config files**: Files which require power to test this includes test data, expected results, database connection variables and any other environmental or test specific details.

- **Third-party API**: Third-party API helps create an optimized test automation framework example. JExcel API to help integrate with Microsoft Excel to create a data driven framework.

- **Selenium**: Selenium JARs to be used for UI automation.

- **SoapUI Runner**: This is used to run the SoapUI project and is a very useful utility for test automation as it allows you to run the test from the command line and acts as a trigger for test automation.

- **Groovy**: This library is used to enable SoapUI to provide its users with groovy as a scripting language.

- **Properties**: Test request properties to hold any dynamically generated data. We also have Test properties to configure SSL and other security configurations for test requests.

- **Test Report**: SoapUI provides a Junit style report and user Jasper reporting utility for reporting of test results.

Test architecture in detail

SoapUI Architecture is composed of many key components which help provide the users of SoapUI with advanced functionality like virtualization, XPath, invoking services with JMS endpoints, logging, and debugging.

Let's discuss these key components in detail:

- **Jetty**: Service virtualization/mock services
  - ° We can create replicas of services in cases where the service is not ready or buggy to test. In the meantime, we want to create our test cases, for that we can use service virtualization or mocking and use that service.
  - ° Jetty is used for hosting virtual services.
  - ° Provided by Eclipse, Java based web server.
  - ° Works for both SOAP and Rest.

- **Jasper**:
  - ° Is used to generate reports
  - ° Open source reporting tool

- **Saxon XSLT and XQuery processor**:
  - ° We can use Path and XQuery to process service results
  - ° The Saxon platform provides us with the option to process results using Path and XQuery

- **Log4J**:
  - ° Used for logging
  - ° Provides SoapUI, error, HTTP, Jetty, and memory logs

- **JDBC driver**:
  - ° To interact with different databases we would need the respective drivers

- **Hermes MS**:
    - ° Is used in applications where high volume of transactions take place
    - ° It is used to send messages to the JMS Queue
    - ° Receiver results from the JMS Queue
    - ° We can incorporate Java JMS using Hermes JMS

- **Scripting language**:
    - ° We can choose with Groovy or JavaScript
    - ° We can select language for each project
    - ° We can set language at project property level

- **Monitoring:**
    - ° To check what is sent to the service and what is received from the service

- **Runners:**
    - ° Execution can be run without using SoapUI
    - ° Run from the command line
    - ° Test runner
    - ° LoadTestRunner
    - ° SecurityTestRunner
    - ° MockServiceRunner
    - ° Can also be executed from build tools such as Jenkins

Test approaches in SOA testing

Approaches to test SOA architecture are usually based on the scope of the project and requirements to test. Let's look at an example.

Following is a diagram of a three-tier architecture based on SOA architecture:

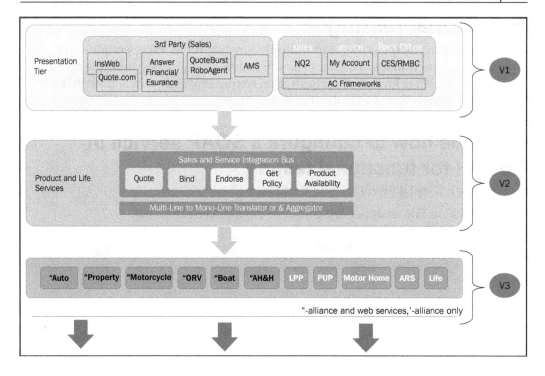

- **Validation1 or V1**: Validation of integration between **Presentation Layer** to the **Services Layer**
- **Validation2 or V2**: Validation of integration between **Services Layer** to the **Service Catalogue Layer**
- **Validation3 or V3**: Validation of integration between Product catalogue layer and the database or backend Layer

So we have three integration points which makes us understand that we need integration testing also with functional, performance and security testing. So let's sum up the types of testing that are required to test end-to-end Greenfield projects.

- Functional testing
- Integration testing
- Performance testing
- Security testing
- Automation testing

Functional testing

A web service may expose single or multiple functionalities via operations and sometimes we need to test a business flow which requires calling multiple services in sequence which is known as orchestration testing in which we validate that a particular business flow meets the requirement.

Let's see how to configure a SOAP service in SoapUI for functional testing

1. Open SoapUI by clicking on the launch icon.

2. Click on **File** in upper-left corner of the top navigation bar.

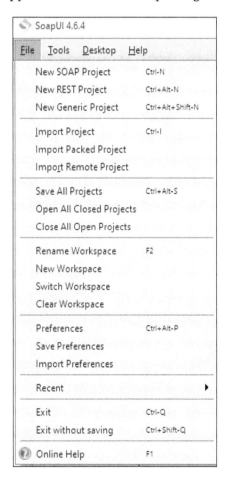

3. Click on **New SOAP Project** heading in the **File** menu.

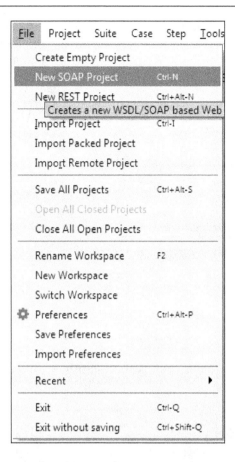

4. Verify that a popup opens up which asks for the WSDL or WADL details. There are two ways you can pass a URL to the web location of the WSDL, or you can pass a link to the downloaded WSDL on your local system.

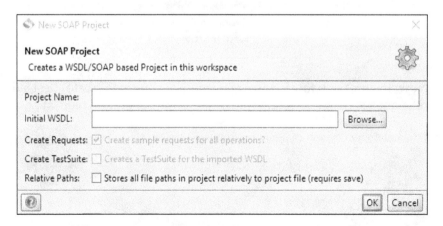

5. Enter the project name details and the WSDL location which can either be on your local machine or be called from a URL, then click on **OK**. You may verify that the WSDL is successfully loaded in SoapUI with all the operations.

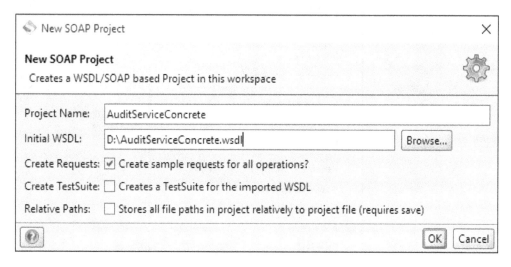

6. Now you can see that service is successfully loaded in the workspace of SoapUI.

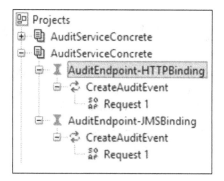

7. Now, the first step toward an organized test suite is to create a test suite and relevant test cases. To achieve this, click on the operation request:

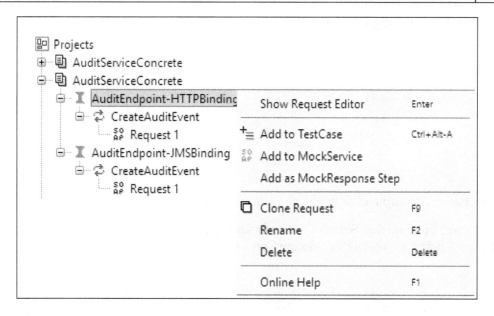

8. When you click on **Add to TestCase** you are asked for the test suite name and then a test case name and finally you will be presented with the following popup:

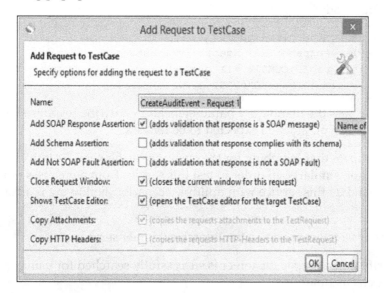

Here you can create a TestCase and add validations to it at run time.

9. After clicking **OK** you are ready to start your functional and integration testing:

Let's take an example of how to test a simple web service functionally.

Test case: Validate that Search Customer searches for the customer from the system database using an MSISDN (Telecom Service).

 Please note MSISDN is a unique identifier for a user to be searched in the database and is a mandatory parameter.

API to be tested, Search Customer:

- Request body:

```
<v11:SearchCustomerRequest>
    <v11:username>TEST_Agent1</v11:username>
    <v11:orgID>COM01</v11:orgID>
    <v11:MSISDN>447830735969</v11:MSISDN>
```

So to test it we pass the mandatory parameters and verify the response which should get us the response parameters expected to be fetched.

By this we validate that searching for the customer using some Search criteria is successful or not, similarly, in order to test this service from a business point of view we need to validate this service with multiple scenarios. Following is a list of a few of them.

Considering it's a telecom application search customer service:

- Verify that a prepay customer is successfully searched for using Search customer
- Verify that a post-pay customer is successfully searched for using Search customer
- Verify that agents are successfully searched for using search customer

- Verify that the results retrieved in response have the right data
- Verify that all the mandatory parameters are presenting the response of the service

Here is how the response looks:

Response Search Customer

<TBD>

Previous are some examples of Priority1 scenarios that you will require to test this service we will give it a deeper look in the following chapters.

Performance testing

So is it really possible to perform performance testing in SoapUI?

The answer is yes, if you just want to do a very simple test on your service itself, not on the orchestration.

SoapUI does have limitations when it comes to performance testing but it does provide you a functionality to generate load on your web service with different strategies.

So to start with, once you have created your SoapUI project for a service operation, you can just convert the same to a simple load test. Here is how:

1. Right-click on the **Load Test** option available:

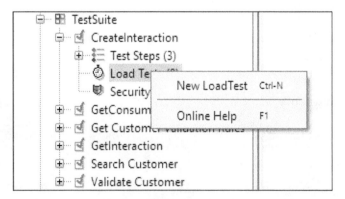

2. Now select the name of the load test; a more relevant one will help you in future runs.

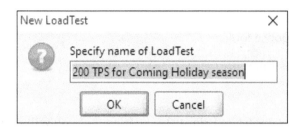

3. You will now see that the load test popup appears and the load test is created:

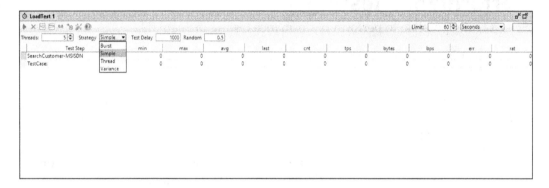

4. There are several strategies to generate load in SoapUI. The strategies are as follows:

- **Simple**
- **Burst**
- **Thread**
- **Variance**

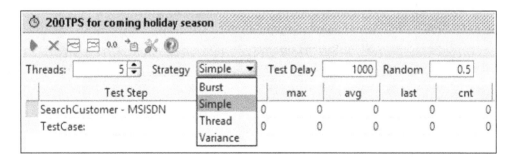

We will learn more about performance testing using SoapUI in the following chapters.

Security testing

API and web services are highly vulnerable to security attacks and we need to be absolutely sure about the security of the exposed web service depending on the architecture of the web service and the nature of its use.

Some of the common attacks types include the following:

- Boundary attack
- Cross-site scripting
- XPath injection
- SQL injection
- Malformed XML
- XML bomb
- Malicious attachment

SoapUI's security testing functionality provides scans for every attack type and also, if you want to try a custom attack on the service by writing a custom script.

So the scans provided by SoapUI are as follows:

- Boundary scan
- Cross-site scripting scan
- XPath injection scan
- SQL injection scan
- Malformed XML scan
- XML bomb scan
- Malicious attachment scan
- Fuzzing scan
- Custom script

Following are the steps for how we configure a security test in SoapUI:

1. You can see an option for **Security Tests** just below Load Tests in SoapUI.

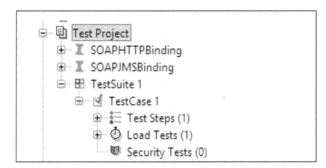

2. To add a test, right-click on the **Security Tests** and select **New SecurityTest**:

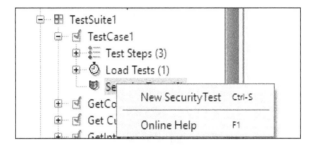

3. Now select **New SecurityTest** and verify that a popup asking the name of the security test opens:

4. Select the name of the security test and click on **OK**.

5. After that, you should see the security test configuration window opened on the screen. For the service operation of your test case, in case of multiple operation in the same test case, you can configure for multiple operations in a single security test as well.

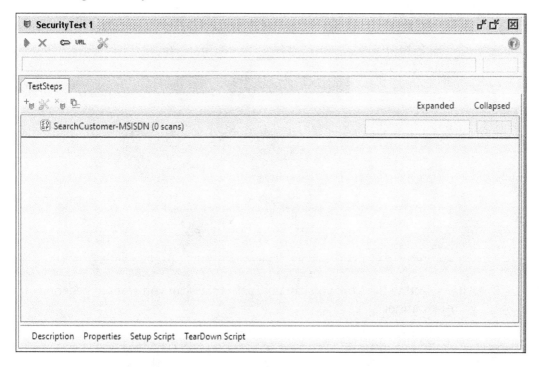

For this pane you can select and configure scans on your service operations.

6. To add a scan, click on the selected icon in the following screenshot:

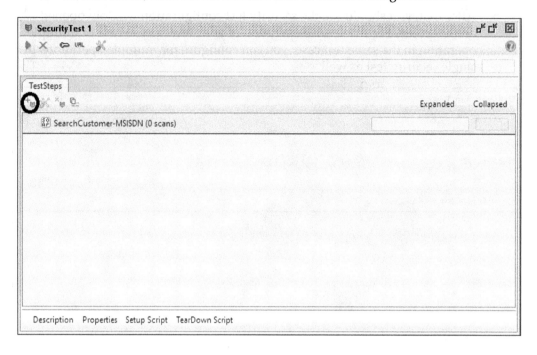

7. After selecting the icon, you can now select the scan you want to generate on your operation:

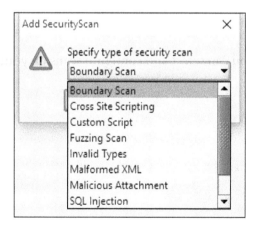

8. After that you can configure your scan for the relevant parameter by configuring the XPath of the parameter in the request.

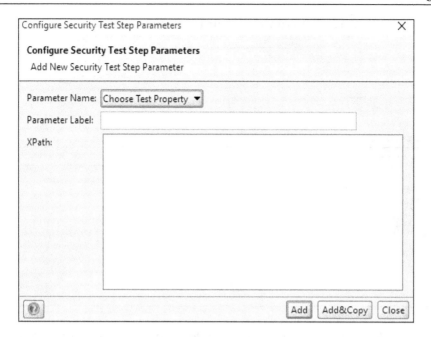

9. After that you can select **Assertions** and **Strategy** tabs from the below options:

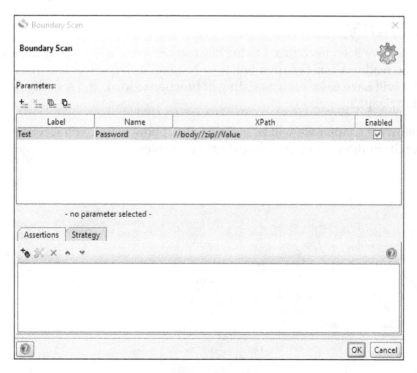

10. You are now ready to run you security test with **Boundary Scan**:

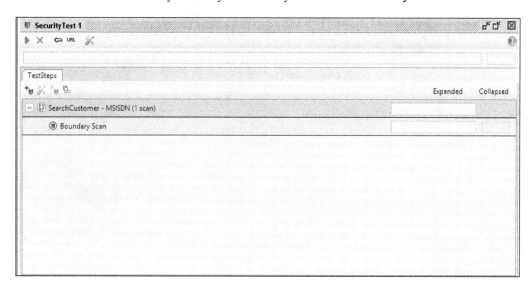

Now we have learnt how to configure a simple security test in SoapUI, we will learn more about it in detail in the coming chapters.

Summary

So now we have been introduced to the key features of SoapUI and by the end of this chapter the readers of this chapter will now be familiar with SOA and SOA Testing. They now will have basic understanding of functional, load, and security testing in SOA using SoapUI.

In the following chapter we will be learning about how to test web services and web service orchestration in detail with real-time examples

2
Functional Testing In Detail

In the previous chapter we learnt how to configure SoapUI to test the services functionally, in this chapter we will cover the following topics in detail

- Service orchestration and testing it using SoapUI
- Assertions
- Configuring SoapUI for JMS Services using Hermes JMS
- Real time example of testing a service orchestration

Service orchestration

When services act in a manner that serves a business purpose which results in a business process being completed, it's known as service orchestration. It directly addresses the implementation of business process implementation. It actually binds business logic and data exchange between applications together so that the desired flow is met.

From another point of view, it can also be said that service orchestration arranges services so that they look like a single service meant to complete a single flow.

To achieve service orchestration, every service involved in orchestration shares data among themselves where sometimes an output of one service acts as an input to the other.

But it should be noted that individual services are not designed to communicate with each other, messages should be exchanged based on certain business rules and execution sequence. To provide communication between all applications in SOA we have the concept of **Enterprise Application Integration (EAI)**. It's more like a framework which utilizes software and systems together to achieve data and business process communication.

It should also be noted that EAI defines a set of principles for integration of multiple systems for communication architectures, such as message-oriented middleware and so on.

To understand more, let's take an example of service orchestration in a telecom application:

A new user install in a telecom application

A user needs a new sim card for voice calling and data so he submits his details to the agent.

Now let's see what happens behind the UI layer:

1. The agent logs in to the UI and submits user information.
2. A defaulters check is made on the user details to check for previously disputed records with the telecom service provider. If the response of the service is yes, then the process stops and the user is notified.
3. A serviceability check is made on the user's address by a service to make sure that the services requested are available. If the response of the service is no, the process stops and the agent is notified else we move forward.
4. A call is made to the product service, which in turns calls the product catalogue to get the product to price mapping, and comes up with the price list for the services asked.
5. Finally, the order is submitted to the provisioning service and once provisioned, the services are activated with the defined SLA.

In the preceding example we see how the orchestrated services talk to each other, pass data to each other, process it, and finally complete the journey of a new order.

As the preceding example illustrates, service orchestration is a fundamental aspect of successfully implementing SOA. In a truly service-oriented architecture, new applications are created by new orchestrations of existing services - not by writing new code.

We have now seen that service orchestration is complex and it requires exchange of data and information among several services, databases, and third-party systems to achieve the desired functional behavior.

So how do we go about testing it?

Key features of SoapUI to test service orchestration

Before we learn how to test service orchestration scenarios in SoapUI let's see some of the functionalities of SoapUI which would help us in testing service orchestration and also help us in automating service orchestration flows.

Dynamic data generation

In several instances, we would need to pass dynamic data each time we enter data in a request, for example, every time we register a customer there needs to be a unique phone number, maybe with a specified format. If you are automating your test you need a technique to generate it each time without any manual intervention.

For this we can use the functionality of groovy scripts in SoapUI. Now let's see how to add a groovy script in SoapUI:

[Pre-requisite: You have already added a Test Suite and a Test case in SoapUI in your own project.]

1. Go to **Test Steps**. Right-click on it and verify that the following screen is shown:

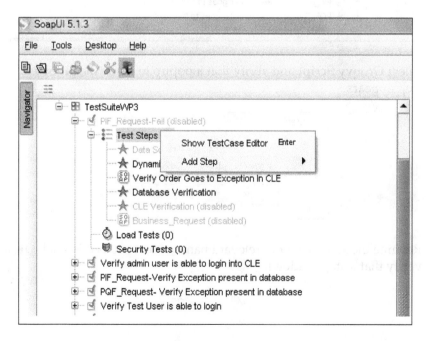

2. Select **Add Step** from the screen and verify the following options are shown:

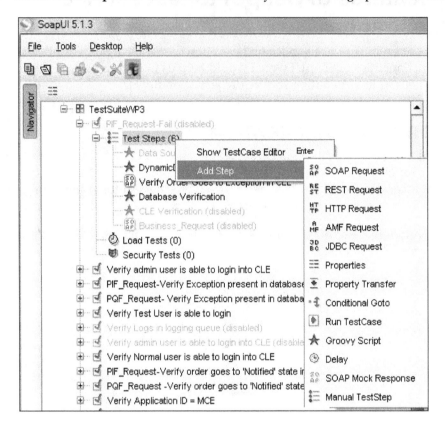

3. Select **Groovy Script** and verify that a popup to name the groovy step appears:

4. Rename the step to a more relevant name or leave it as it is, click **OK** and verify that a step is added.

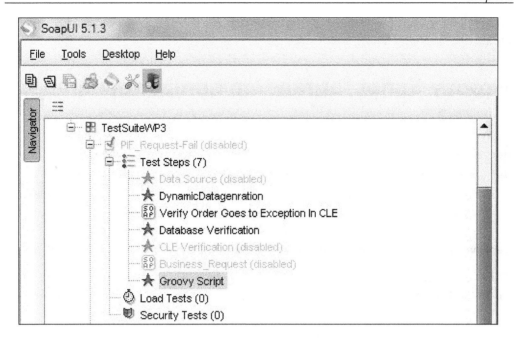

5. Double-click on the **Groovy Script** and the following script console will be displayed:

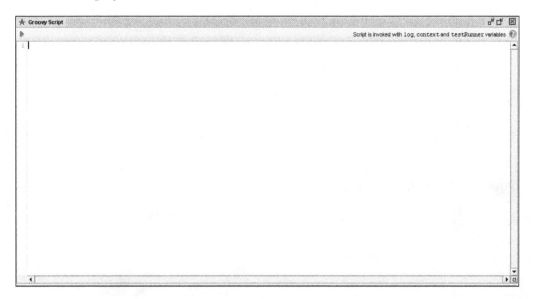

Now we have seen how to add a groovy test step in SoapUI, let's now see how to create dynamic data using groovy script:

Groovy Script for random number generation

Following is the script which will create unique data for you to be used each time the test is executed:

```
def PhoneNumber1=(Math.round(Math.random()*9977777770)+0000000010);

def ProductId =(Math.round(Math.random()*99999999990000)+10000000010);

testRunner.testCase.setPropertyValue("PhoneNumber",PhoneNumber1.toString
());


testRunner.testCase.setPropertyValue("ProductID",ProductId.toString ());
```

This script creates unique data to be used by a request each time you run it. This script saves the data in the properties at the test case level. See the screenshot that follows:

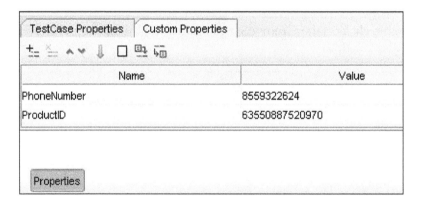

Then from any request you can call this data. The properties can be called from any request in the project/test suite:

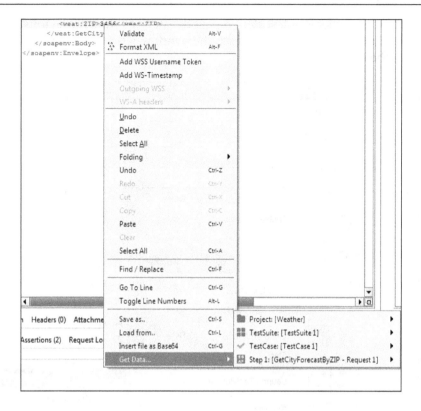

The important thing to note here is that we can save the data at each level based on our requirements, for instance at the test suite level, test case level, and project level there are options to save custom properties.

Property transfer

We have seen in our pre examples that in service orchestration, response parameter data of one service may become essential for the other service. Therefore, we would need to transfer the necessary data from a response to another request. To achieve the data transfer between services we use property transfer.

To add property transfer as a test step, repeat the steps as shown previously to add a groovy script and finally, when you reach the window where you have all the steps listed, select the following step:

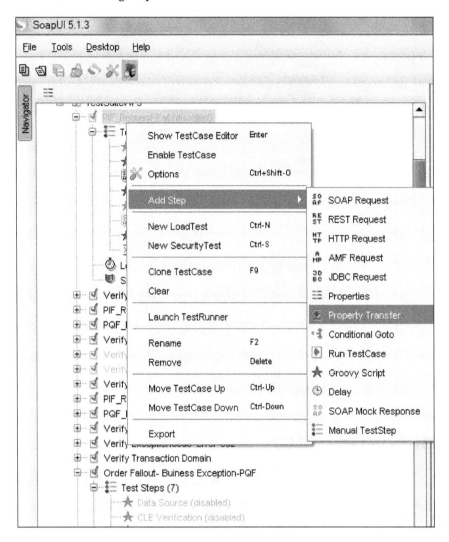

You will then find the **Property Transfer** configuration window:

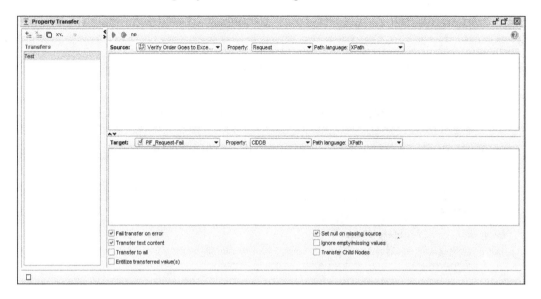

In the preceding window you need to configure the following:

- **Source**: Test step which is the source of the data to be transferred
- **Property**: Usually the response which has the response parameter data to be transferred
- **Path language**: XPath for a single node of the same parameter name, X query for a multiple data set with the same parameter name, and JSON for a REST API using JSON message exchange format
- **Target**: The target which requires the data extracted
- **Property** in the **Target** section: Property which is used to consume the extracted value from the source
- **Path language** in the **Target** section: This can be XPath, XQuery, or JSON based on your requirements.

Property transfer is a critical step when automating orchestrations as we require frequent data exchange between services.

Assertions

Assertions are validations which are used to validate whether the system is working as expected or not.

SoapUI provides you with a variety of assertions, let's have a look at each one of them by category:

- **Property Content**: This assertion type is used to validate the parameter data returned in response by the service

    ◦ **XPath Match**: This assertion is used to match a particular node value in the response with the expected values

○ **XQuery Match**: When you want to validate multiple sets of values from the response, XQuery Match is used to validate multiple parameters of data in the response in a single assertion

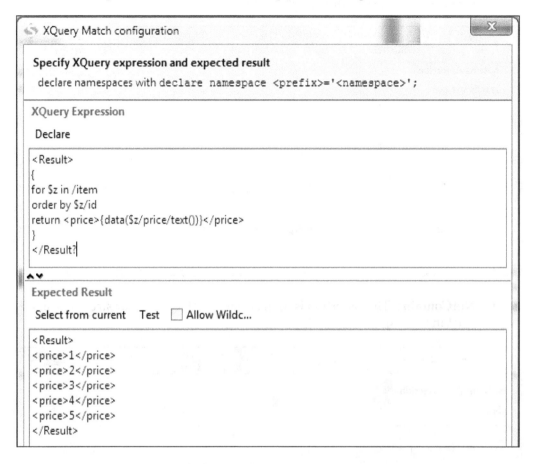

In the preceding example there is an XML which has multiple price tags and the tester wants to retrieve all the prices from an XML response.

So the XQuery searches in every item and returns all the prices for each Item.

- **Contains**: This assertion is used to validate if a particular value or string exists in the response or supports wildcards

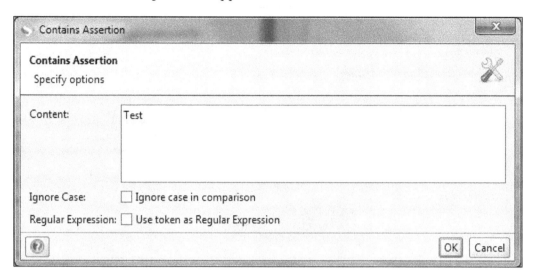

- **NotContains**: This assertion is to make sure that a particular string doesn't exist in the response

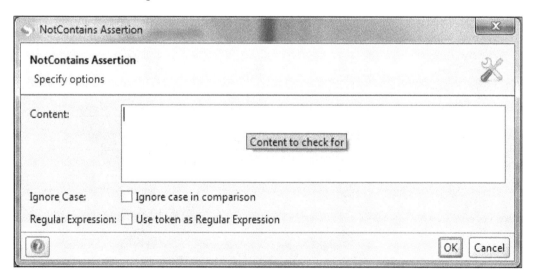

- **Compliance status and standards**: This Assertion type is used to validate whether the returned status code or fault code adheres to the expected value or not

- **Invalid HTTP status codes**: This Assertion validates whether the returned HTTP Code adheres to the expected value or not

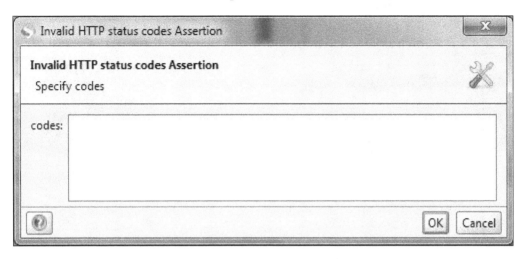

- **Not SOAP Fault**: This Assertion validates that the response received from the service is not a SOAP fault

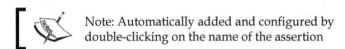 Note: Automatically added and configured by double-clicking on the name of the assertion

- **Schema Compliance**: This Assertion validates that the received message is compliant with the WSDL or not

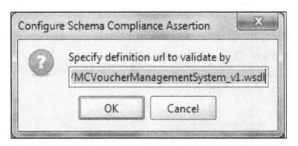

- **SOAP Fault**: This assertion validates that the response received is a soap fault or not

Note: Automatically added and configured by double clicking on the name of the assertion

- **Script**: Script assertions are used to create any custom assertion with the help of groovy script
  - ○ **Script Assertion**: Script assertion is the best way to implement your own assertion to meet your requirements

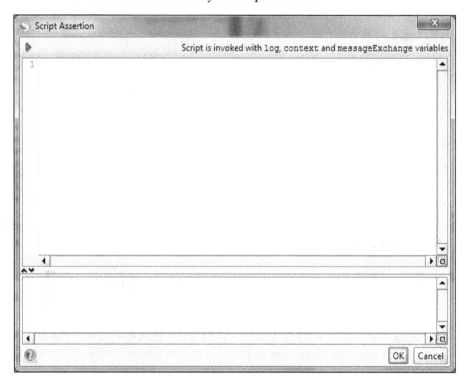

- **Response SLA**: This Type of assertion is to validate the response time
  - ○ **Response SLA Assertion**: This assertion is to validate the response time of the service and may be used to verify the performance of the service at the initial stages

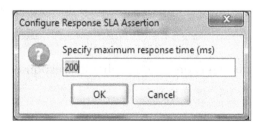

- **JMS**: This type of assertion is to for services exposed over the JMS protocol.

  ○ **JMS Status**: This Assertion is to validate if the message is posted on the queue or not

 This assertion is automatically added and configured

  ○ **JMS Timeout**: This assertion is to validate that the time of execution for the JMS statement is no longer than expected.

 This Assertion is automatically added and configured

- **Security**:

  ○ **Sensitive Information Exposure**: This assertion is to make sure that any confidential information like usernames, passwords or server IP is not exposed in the response of the service of which any hacker or intruder may take advantage

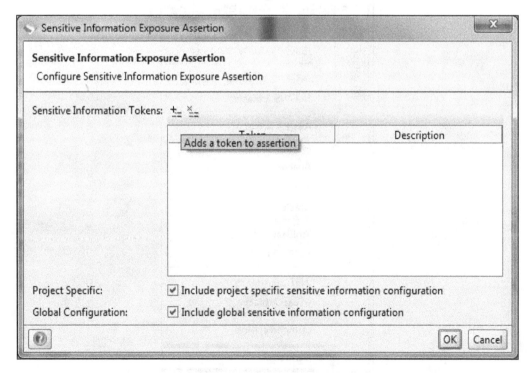

That was all about assertions in SoapUI however, when we need a customized assertion we always have the power of groovy script to create our own and achieve our desired functionality.

Configuring SoapUI for JMS services using Hermes JMS

Web services use multiple protocols for transport, for example, HTTP or JMS. Communication can also be different, for example, Soap or JSON. So let's go configure JMS for different middleware like Tibco,Oracle SOA, IBM WebSphere.

To configure JMS in SoapUI we have a utility called Hermes JMS to help us configure JMS in our test.

Following are the steps to configure Hermes JMS in SoapUI:

1.   Open **HermesJMS** from the **Tools** option on the top and select **HermesJMS**:

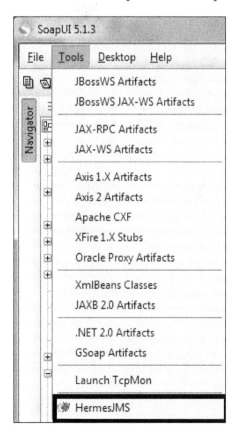

2. Verify that **HermesJMS** will open on your desktop:

3. Configuring a session: Select a **New Session**:

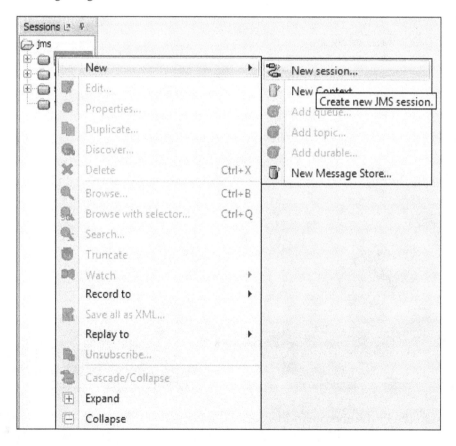

4. Configuring a **New session**: On selection of a new session, verify that the **Preferences** window comes up:

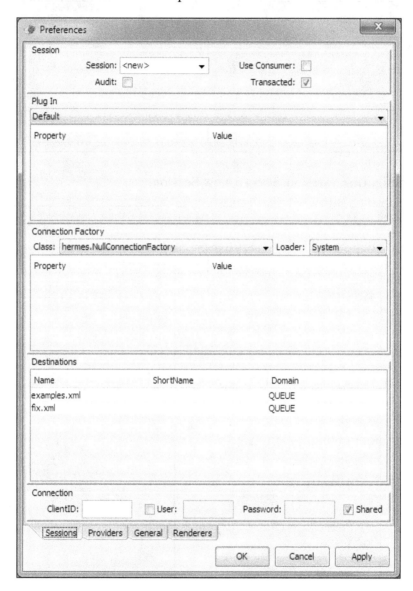

5. On the **Preferences** window select the **Providers** tab.

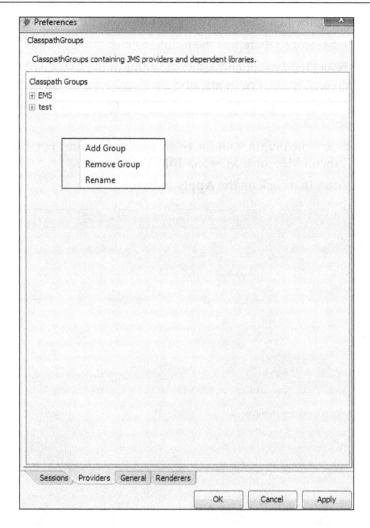

6. On selection of a **New Group** add the **Jars** based on the middleware used, for example, for Tibco, use the following JARS:
   ° Tibemsd.JAR
   ° Tibjms.jar
   ° Tibjmsadmin.jar

7. For Active MQ use the following:
   ° com.ibm.mq.pcf-6.1.jar
   ° com.ibm.mq.jar
   ° com.ibm.mqjms.jar
   ° dhbcore.jar
   ° connector.jar

8. After adding the Jars click on **Apply** and move to the **Sessions** tab.

9. From the **Sessions** tab, repeat the following steps in the following sequence:

    1. Select the **Loader** and select the name of the Class path group you created in the **Providers** tab.

    2. Select **Class:Com.tibco.tibjms.TibjmsQueueConnectionFactory** for TIBCO.

    3. Select the plugin with the relevant **Plugin** name. For Tibco, select **Tibco EMS**; for IBM, select **IBM WebSphere**.

    4. After that click on the **Apply** button.

10. On the left hand pane, select the session name provided and right click on it.

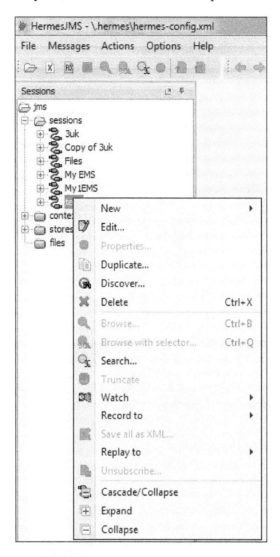

11. Select the **Discover** option. You will then have all of the queues discovered.

12. Open SoapUI and move to the binding of the JMS service and right click on it.

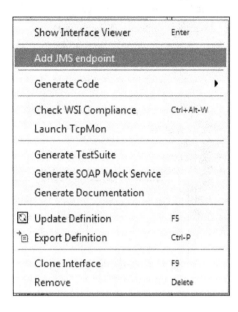

13. On selecting to **Add JMS endpoint** you will be routed to the **Add JMS endpoint** window:

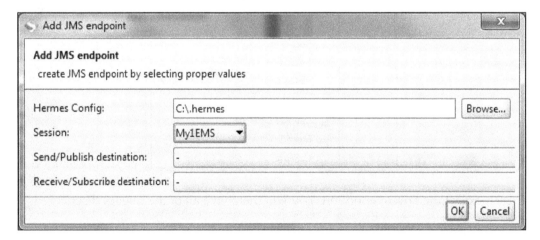

14. Select the **Session** and then the **Send Queue** from the list of the queues:

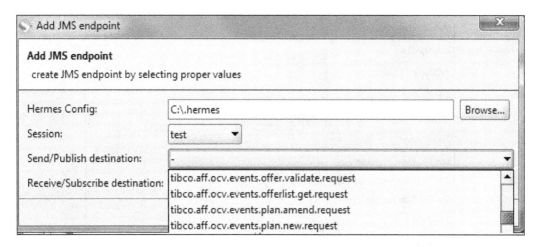

Now let's take an example of configuring the request for JMS messages:

1. Open the request and configure the endpoint with the queue name and then add `::queue_` at the end of the queue. So any JMS endpoint in SoapUI would be like the following:

   ```
   Jms//session name::sendingQueue::receiving queue
   ```

   Here you are having `queue_` as a temporary queue in SoapUI to receive the response and acting as a receiving queue.

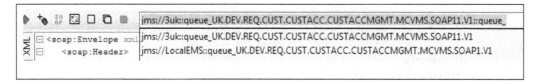

2. Select the two checkboxes from the JMS headers option:

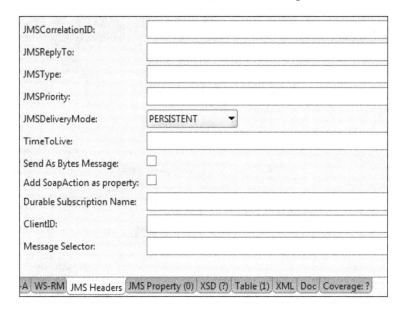

Let's have a look at the options shown in the preceding screenshot:

*   **JMSCorrelationID**: This is used to map the request and response message in a transaction
*   **JMSReplyTo**: This describes the queue or a topic to which the response must be sent
*   **JMSType**: This field indicates the nature of the message enumeration may vary based on the JMS vendor
*   **JMSPriority**: The priority at which the message is sent range varies from 0 to 9 with 0 as least, and 9 as most important
*   **JMSDeliveryMode**: It has two enumerations:
    *   **PERSISTENT**: Message is stored in a store
    *   **NON PERSISTENT**: Message is not stored in a store
*   **TimeToLive**: The time the message should exist on the queue till
*   **Send As Bytes Message**: This option, when selected, sends the message as bytes
*   **Add SoapAction as property**: This option when checked adds SoapAction to the request
*   **Durable Subscription Name**: Name of the durable subscription

- **ClientID**: Used to uniquely identify any durable subscriber
- **Message Selector**: Allows you to filter the messages that a Message Consumer will receive

After this you can successfully launch a test against all JMS services.

You can also use the script from the following section to send any JMS messages on a destined queue.

Groovy script

This groovy script lets you create a JMS endpoint and sends messages to queues using Groovy script:

```
import com.eviware.soapui.impl.wsdl.submit.transports.jms.
JMSConnectionHolder;
import com.eviware.soapui.impl.wsdl.submit.transports.jms.util.
HermesUtils;
import com.eviware.soapui.impl.wsdl.submit.transports.jms.JMSEndpoint;
import hermes.Hermes;
import javax.jms.*;
def jmsEndpoint = new  JMSEndpoint("jms://activeMQSession::queue_
testQ1::queue_testQ1");
def hermes = HermesUtils.getHermes( context.testCase.testSuite.
project, jmsEndpoint.sessionName);
def jmsConnectionHolder = new JMSConnectionHolder( jmsEndpoint,
hermes, false, null ,null ,null);
Session queueSession = jmsConnectionHolder.getSession();
Queue queueSend = jmsConnectionHolder.getQueue( jmsConnectionHolder.
getJmsEndpoint().getSend() );
Queue queueBrowse = jmsConnectionHolder.getQueue( jmsConnectionHolder.
getJmsEndpoint().getReceive() );
MessageProducer messageProducer =queueSession.createProducer(
queueSend );
TextMessage textMessageSend = queueSession.createTextMessage();
textMessageSend.setText( "jms message from groovy");
messageProducer.send( textMessageSend );
textMessageSend.setText( "another jms message from groovy");
messageProducer.send( textMessageSend );
QueueBrowser qb  = queueSession.createBrowser(queueBrowse);
Enumeration en= qb.getEnumeration();
while(en.hasMoreElements()){
    TextMessage tm = (TextMessage)en.nextElement();
    log.info tm.getText()
    }
jmsConnectionHolder.closeAll()// don't forget to close session and
connection
```

End-to-end demonstration of testing an orchestrated flow

Testing an orchestrated flow is very interesting in SoapUI and the tools help you a lot while also automating your end-to-end flow. Let's take an example of a service orchestration in a stock management application:

- **Example**: The application has five APIs for maintaining stock
- **Get Stock Availability**: Get the availability of the stock
- **Reserve Stock**: Reserve the Stock if the stock is available
- **Commit Reservation**: Finally commit a reservation based on the reservation ID received from the reserve stock response
- **Validate Reservation**: Validate whether the reservation commit was successful or not
- **Cancel Reservation**: Cancel a reservation
- **Scenario1**: Canceling a reserved stock and verifying if the stock gets added in the available stock list or not.
    - ° **Call1**: Get stock Availability: This returns the availability of the stock with the number of quantities available

Validations on the call:

- **V1**: Verify that the number of Quantities Returned are in sync in the database
- **V2**: Verify that the quantities of stocks are adjusted automatically when a reservation is cancelled or when a stock is reserved

Following are the SoapUI screenshots for a more detailed look.

Get Stock Availability: We now will trigger this call for a specific product ID and location and see the status for a product and its availability:

```
<v11:GetStockAvailabilityResponse>
        <v11:Stocks>
            <!--1 or more repetitions:-->
            <v11:Stock>
                <v11:productID>10111</v11:productID>
                <v11:locationID>890</v11:locationID>
                <v11:stockStatus>INSTOCK</v11:stockStatus>

                <!--You may enter ANY elements at this point-->
            </v11:Stock>
        </v11:Stocks>
    </v11:GetStockAvailabilityResponse>
```

So now we see in the preceding screenshot that that product is available and we have 385 quantities for this item.

Let's now go ahead and reserve it.

Reserve Stock: We will now reserve the same stock for which we did a get stock availability call.

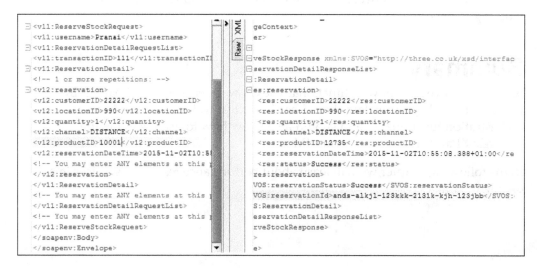

Retriggering Get Stock Availability:

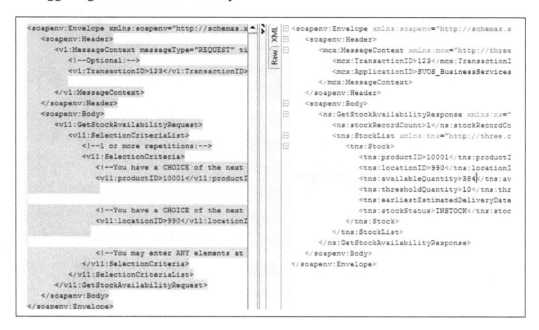

We can now see that the available quantity has decreased by 1, this then proves that the orchestration between Get Stock Availability and Reserve stock is working as expected.

Summary

So now we have seen how to functionally test a web service using SoapUI. By the end of the chapter readers should be able to test web services and service orchestration functionality and should also know how to use the following features: XPath, Assertions, HermesJMS.

In the following chapter we will learn about performance testing of services in a detailed manner.

3

Performance Testing of SOA Applications in Detail

In the previous chapter we learnt about functional testing of web services in detail. In this chapter we will go through the following topics:

- Performance testing in the SOA world.
- Performance test planning.
- SoapUI load generation techniques.
- Real-time example of performance testing on web services
- Analysis of performance results
- SoapUI and LoadUI integration

Performance testing in the SOA world

Performance testing in an SOA application is done a bit differently compared to any other architecture. We don't just need to validate performance requirements of single service components but also test the orchestration, as well as the third-party services.

We can categorize performance testing in the following way:

- Component level
- Scenario level
- System level

Let's go through them in detail.

Component level: When we test the performance of a particular service in isolation it is known as component level performance testing.

Here we test if the response time of the service is within acceptable limits and we also analyze the behavior of the service under different types of performance tests.

This type of performance test is helpful to evaluate the performance of the service in isolation and we get the results early.

We can perform this type of testing easily using SoapUI. We will see this in the coming sections.

Scenario level: When we are done with component level testing and have identified and rectified the performance bottlenecks, the next step is to identify a critical business process to validate.

We aim to verify whether the given business flows, which are achieved via orchestration, are achieved within the acceptable performance measurements.

For example, a new customer order from a retail website will involve multiple service invocations and interaction with multiple databases and third party systems.

Our objective here is to verify the performance of the business tested under varied load conditions.

If the test took more time than expected, a root cause analysis is done to identify any performance bottlenecks like memory leakage, disk usage, and so on.

This type of testing requires a monitoring tool to be set up on the servers which can be used to identify the bottlenecks.

System level: A system level test focuses on putting the load on the architecture of the application and verifying the performance of the architecture under peak load.

To put the load at system level it is advisable to identify the following pre-requisites:

- Work load model
- Areas of probable pain
- Scenarios for work load model
- User distribution as per the scenario
- Performance counters to be monitored
- Monitoring tools to be placed on the servers
- In case of third-party services, stubs need to be created

Also it should be noted that if the load balancer is in place we should target the load to the load balancer URL.

Once all the prerequisites have been identified and met we are now good to start system level performance testing.

It can be difficult to identify performance bottlenecks in an SOA solution if we have not first done a component level and scenario level performance test.

The analysis phase is the last and most complex phase in system level performance testing as we have multiple performance counters to monitor and analyze.

We should also take into account the third-party services, components, and systems which would be difficult to performance test and analyze. The reason for why it is difficult to analyze the performance of third party systems is because those services are rarely available to us before production, and we can only stub them till then, we should therefore isolate such services and create stubs of those services.

A solution to this issue is to make sure that the third Party services don't become a bottleneck for the system and should be mocked or virtualized effectively. The Third Party vendor can also share his performance results and then a comparison can be made in case of any conflicts by running a test on the virtualized environment and the performance numbers shared by third party vendors.

Apart from this solution, we can request the client or third-party vendor to provide us with a replica of production.

 Note: We will study the details of the performance prerequisites in the following chapters.

Let's go through some famous tools in the open source arena for performance testing:

- **SoapUI**: SoapUI is an open source tool that can be used for web service testing. In addition to functional testing, SoapUI can also be used for performance testing. One of the advantages of using SoapUI is that you can use it to perform security testing.

- **LoadUI**: LoadUI is an open source tool from SmartBear and is used for measuring performance of your SOA applications. It supports almost all protocols except for JMS.

- **Apache JMeter**: JMeter is an open source tool that can be used for analyzing and measuring performance and performing REST/SOAP invocations. This tool can be used to automate most user stories. It allows the tester to run the same test with different users and also has the ability to perform parameterization. One of the drawbacks of this tool is that it cannot be used to automate security-related scenarios.

- **cURL**: cURL is a command line tool that is used to send or retrieve information with the use of URL syntax. This tool supports many Internet protocols such as HTTP, HTTPS, FTP, IMAP, and many more. cURL is not heavily used for load testing and is mainly used for functional testing.

Now let's go through some of famous Monitoring tools – the following are Open Source:

- **JConsole**: JConsole is a graphical monitoring tool that is used to monitor **Java Virtual Machine (JVM)** and Java applications, both on local and on remote machines.
- **JProfiler**: The JProfiler can be used to identify performance bottlenecks, pin down memory leaks, and understand threading issues.

We also have lots of very good commercial tools for performance testing in SOA space:

- SoapUI Pro or Ready API
- Load Runner
- LoadUI pro
- SOA Parasoft
- ITKO LISA

Performance test planning

Planning a performance test is the most important part of performance testing. Let's take a deeper look at it. The very first thing in planning a performance test is analysis:

- **Analysis phase**: This phase predominantly focuses and summarizes in detail the analysis and findings which will underpin the performance test of the systems to validate their ability to handle the forecasted load. During this phase, vendor representatives will be heavily engaged with business and technical representatives to understand and document the historic, current, and anticipated user profiles and projects. The data gathered will be used to model the load profiles and the test data model, at the end of this phase a report will be presented to the stakeholders. The following diagram represents the sequence of events carried out during this phase:

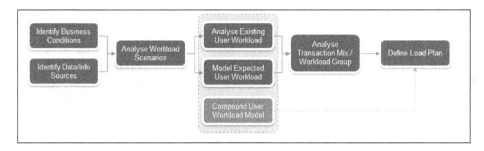

 Note: The terminology used in the diagram will be explained in the coming phases of this section.

- **Delivery phase**: This phase states the methodology to successfully implement performance testing. The core emphasis behind this methodology and its application is to provide stakeholders with a comprehensive view of how the performance objectives will be achieved and the level of assurance that will be delivered, for instance through explanation of any constraints or decisions that could impact the framework and its implementation. This process eliminates overlap and ambiguity in performance testing and provides a detailed plan for implementation, it also aids in de-risking the implementation phase for the performance testing engagement, and the following diagram details the process and its associated deliverables:

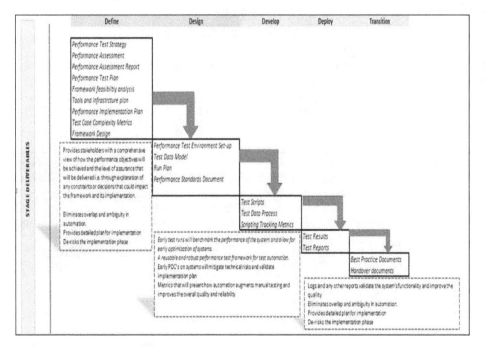

- **WorkLoad model**: In order to successfully execute performance testing, a Workload model will be designed to model the logical set of activities that need to be performed by users (business or customers using the system) towards achieving a certain (business) goal. The main driver behind the workload model has been the Business Workload, where the performance testing team will consider scripting based on the logical set of activities that need to be performed in order to meet the business objectives and goals, different business initiatives that will impact performance of the tool, and the underlying infrastructure.

Types of tests

The following phases of tests will be executed as part of this performance testing effort:

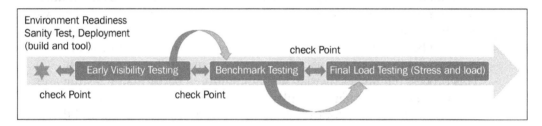

Let's have a look at the various types of performance test types:

Tests	Description
Early Visibility Testing	In this phase the project team gets early visibility of the application's performance, characteristics, and limitations. This phase will encourage feedback on the design, approach, results, and findings. Based on this, decisions can be taken in terms of changing the approach, tools, or even de-scoping certain areas that were made earlier.
Benchmark Testing	A series of tests will be run to benchmark the performance of key processes in a steady state environment. These tests will be used to evaluate and analyze the performance characteristics of the system, the benchmark tests will be run against the same set of data and test scripts that will be used for other stages of the test, these tests are also run to provide early visibility of the system capacity.

Load Testing	A stepped load test to validate the range plan process by taking into account the cumulative increase in member activity: • Apply peak load during week 1 of the creating and planning process • Mix load to include planning for current and next season • Incremental load for read and write queries
Stress Testing	A set of tests to validate increased usage of the system (beyond forecasted level) to determine the system tolerances and capacity

Test execution phase

The test execution phase will follow a streamlined process; the main aim of the process is to review, assess and execute tests in a formal and structured way during the entire duration of the execution phase.

Test execution will only commence when all the entry criteria for a cycle have been met, and will only end when all the exit criteria have been fulfilled and reviewed and mitigating actions for key risks/issues agreed.

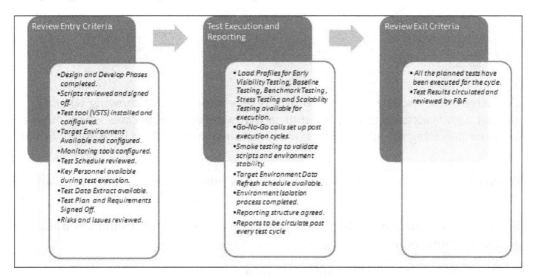

Quality gates

To ensure quality and effectiveness throughout the performance testing program and the integrity of testing it is vital that quality gates are established between phases and that these are formally controlled by the test manager and stakeholders. At the end of each phase of testing, the exit criteria of the phase just completed will be assessed. If these have been fulfilled, then the entry criteria of the succeeding test phase will themselves be assessed in turn before that test phase can be allowed to commence.

The following diagram gives an overview of the quality gates proposed for this testing program:

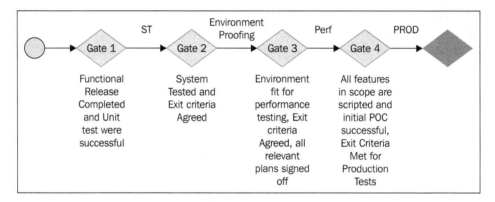

Test environments: The test environment is very important for knowing whether another user is accessing the application at that point in time. In cases where other users are accessing the application at the same time, the results of the test would not be real.

Based on the peak load number, we might need optimal configuration of the load generation machine or we need to use distributed mode for load generation.

Following are sample of the hardware configuration required (the numbers used are sample numbers).

- Hardware configuration of current environment:
    ◦ AMD Quad Core processor @ 2.6 GHz
    ◦ Ram: 'x' GB

- Performance stats collected
    ◦ Peak CPU utilization: 5.1%
    ◦ Peak memory footprint: 145 MB

- Resources required for 100 users

    ° RAM requirements for 100 users test (peak memory footprint: 145MB/5/CPU utilization)*100 = 2900MB ~ 2.84 GB

    ° Considering 80% CPU utilization as optimal for a load generator, we would need 1.28 times the CPU processing of the current machine

Considering the preceding calculations, we can generate a user load of 78 concurrent users using a generator with quad core CPU at 2.6 GHz and 4 GB RAM.

Following are the infrastructure requirements:

- The test environment will need to be established to provide for login and general system access

- Access to the testing systems and applications will need to be established and connections tested

- Servers need to be 100% dedicated to the test during the scheduled times of the test to prevent undue interference from other activities

    ° Each workstation will need to have login and application connections tested prior to performance tests being conducted

Test data: Test data is very important in performance testing. We need to gather the test data or generate it using scripts.

The test data should be unique and should be similar to the data that would be set up in production.

Following is the list of deliverables which are usually required by the client:

Deliverable name	Description
Performance Test Strategy	Provides stakeholders with a comprehensive view of how the performance objectives will be verified and the level of assurance that will be delivered, for instance through explanation of any constraints or decisions that could impact validity of the results.
Performance Test Scripts (multiple)	Describes a set of conditions or variables under which a tester will determine whether an application's performance is acceptable.
Test Schedule	Contains the schedule of testing tasks, activities, and deliverables, along with their associated resource owners. It is used to ensure the testing activities are occurring when planned and there is minimal overlap between test resources.
Performance Test Progress and Scorecard	Describes the performance test's progress during the test's life cycle.

Deliverable name	Description
Performance Test Results	Contains a summarization of Performance Test activities and final results.

Dependency: Following is an example of a dependency list:

ID	Dependency	Description	Impact
1	Pre-Production Build Completed	The pre-production environment should contain a stable and tested build, the emphasis behind this is to minimize any impact on re-work of performance test scripts.	H
2	Pre-Production Access Provided	Access to relevant databases, application is provided to Vendor. Resources would be predominantly used to record the necessary test scripts identified for performance testing.	H
3	Performance Test Tools Deployed/Installed	All the relevant tools are deployed, installed, and smoke tested.	H
4	Test Data requirements agreed	A set of appropriate and valid test data is loaded.	H
5	Early Visibility of build to Pre-Prod	Early indication of the build that is expected to be deployed to pre-production.	M
6	Cycle 1 Test Data Loaded	Test data loaded and sanity tested prior to commencement of cycle 1 testing.	H
7	Drop X Deployed to Pre-Prod	Deployed build successfully completed in pre-production environment, sanity tested and meets the Entry criteria for Cycle 1 test execution.	M

Now that we have taken a detailed look at the Performance testing planning, we should now see how we implement the script creation and implementation using SoapUI.

Performance testing using SoapUI

We have already seen in *Chapter 1, Introduction to SOA Testing*, how to create a performance testing script using SoapUI so let's move on further from there.

We have four load generation strategies in SoapUI:

* Simple
* Thread

- Variance
- Burst

Let's go through each of them in detail.

Simple strategy: This strategy addresses three types of performance test:

- Baseline test
- Load test
- SOAK test

The simple strategy generates a specific amount of virtual user load on the application with a ramp up time between each thread to give breathing space to the application under test.

Following screenshot shows the configuration window where the setting for the simple strategy is set.

The following window is common for each strategy type but works differently for each load generation strategy:

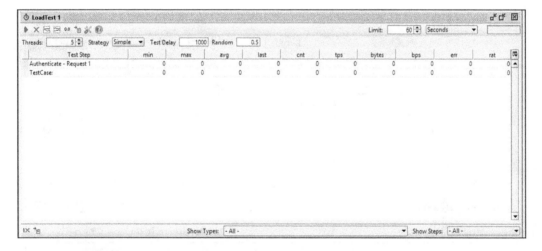

Let's take a detailed look at the previous screenshot:

- **Threads**: To specify the amount of virtual user load on the application in the preceding example we have used five threads which means five virtual users.
- **Test Delay**: The delays you want to keep between each thread, for example 10 threads and 10 sec delay will result in 1 sec wait after each thread.

- **Random**: If you want to vary the wait time, this feature is used. For example, if you put a random of .5 with a delay of 20 seconds then you will have a random delay between threads of 5 to 20 seconds.

- **Limit**: This is for time duration of the Test.

Variance: This technique is used usually for two types of performance testing:

- Recovery testing
- Stress testing

This strategy varies the number of threads over time. Set the **Interval** to the desired value and the Variance to how many the number of threads should decrease and increase.

Let's have a look at the following example.

If we start with **Threads** of **20**, and an **Interval** of **60** and **Variance** of **0.8**, the number of threads will increase from 20 to 36 within the first 15 seconds, then decrease back to 20 and continue down to four threads after 45 seconds, and finally go back up to the initial value after 60 seconds.

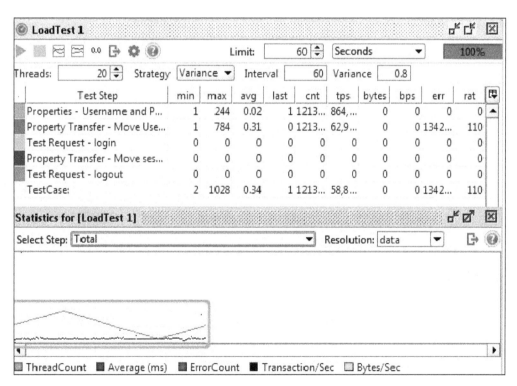

The Variance strategy window has the following options and looks like
the following:

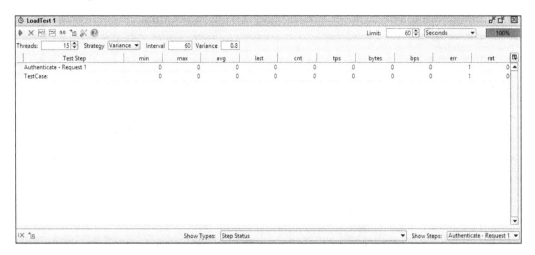

Following are the configuration details:

- **Threads**: The amount of VUser load
- **Interval**: The time after which the threads would start changing up
- **Variance**: The variance defines how much the change would be after the specified set of interval
- **Thread Strategy**: This strategy can be used for the following:
    - Identifying the threshold point
    - Analyzing a particular bottleneck
    - Identifying the load after which functional bugs start to occur

Following is the screenshot which shows the configuration window of the thread strategy:

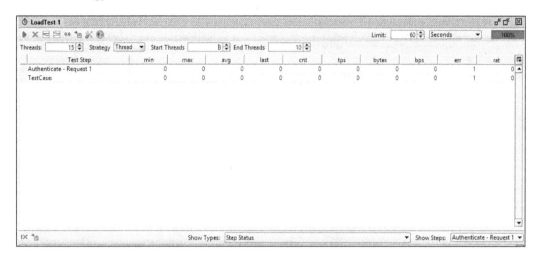

Following are the configuration values of the window:

- **Threads**: Specifies the number of users to run this test case
- **Start Threads**: The number of threads to start the test
- **End Threads**: The number of threads to end the test
- **Limit**: The time till which the test will run in seconds
- **Burst Strategy**: This strategy can be used for the following:
    - Recovery testing
    - Stress testing
    - Bottleneck identification

The burst strategy simulates a scenario where you suddenly have high traffic for some duration on an application. Let's see an example:

In a holiday season, some sites like Amazon give a user more response time than usual because the number of users will be more, similarly a university website at the time of graduation will work much slower than usual as the number of users will peak when the results are announced.

These types of tests are simulated by Burst Strategy. Let's have a look at its configuration window:

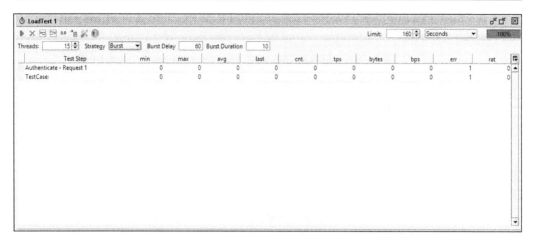

- **Threads**: Specifies the number of threads or VUsers
- **Burst Delay**: Delay between each burst
- **Burst Duration**: The duration of the test

We have now gone through all four types of strategy for load generation using SoapUI. For more advance performance testing we can integrate SoapUI with LoadUI, we will see that in the following sections of this chapter.

Now we know how to generate load on any SOA application, let's see how to validate the response with the help of assertions.

Assertions in performance testing

Assertions can be added by clicking on the icon in the configuration window for each strategy:

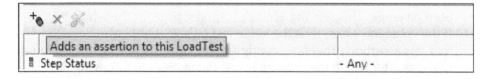

We have the following types of assertions available in the **Add Assertion** panel in the SoapUI window:

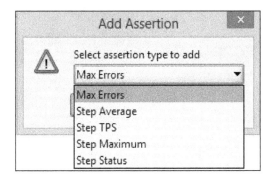

- **Max Errors**: This assertion allows you to configure the maximum number of errors before a load test fails, following is the configuration window:

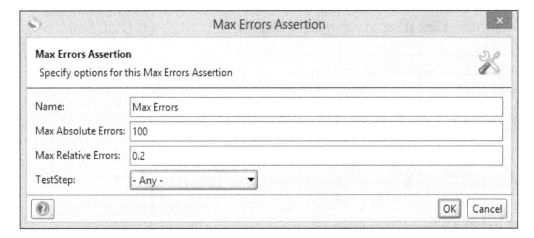

- **Step Average**: This sets the average response time for the whole test. If the value increases, then the value test fails. It should also be noted that this assertion provides a configuration value for setting the minimum requests after which the average is calculated. See the following configuration window:

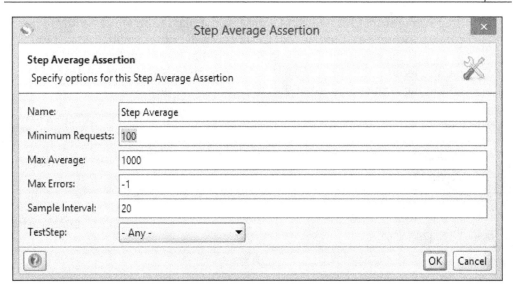

- **Step TPS**: This assertion specifies the desired TPS which the test case should attain and fails if TPS is lower than expected. It should also be noted that there are a minimum number of request configuration parameters after which the TPS calculation is done. The snapshot of the configuration window shown following:

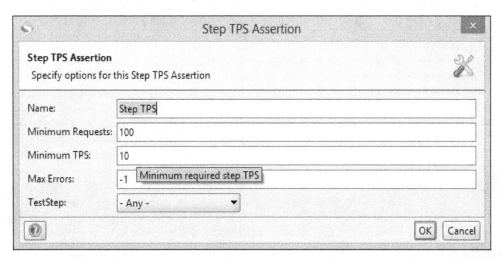

- **Step Maximum**: This assertion validates the maximum value for the corresponding Test Step or Test Case, going over the specified **Max Time** limit fails the assertion. It should be noted that there is a configuration parameter of minimum requests before which, calculation is done. Following is the snapshot of the configuration window:

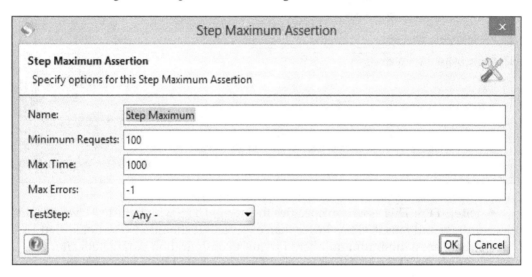

- **Step Status**: Validates whether the underlying test case or test step is executed successfully or not. Following is the configuration window:

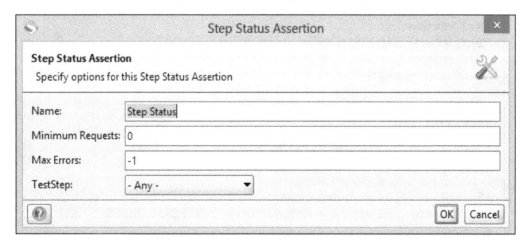

This ends the section for assertion we have now gone through all kinds of load testing assertions which are available in SoapUI.

Analysis

The analysis phase is the last step in the performance test cycle after which we suggest and publish the report to the stakeholder. In this chapter we will study how to capture details of the running test.

In SoapUI we have features to capture data and we have graphs to showcase data which makes it easy to analyze:

The preceding screenshot shows the average thread count over time.

We can select data for **AVERAGE** response time, **TPS, ERRORS** and **BPS** (**Bytes exchanged per second**) as shown in the following screenshot:

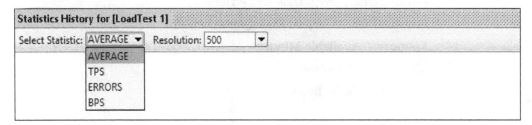

In case we want to monitor the server statistics, we need to switch to monitoring utilities like Perfmon for Windows and SAR and K SAR reporting for Linux-based OSs.

Perfmon: You can access performance monitor by typing `perfmon` at the command prompt or by selecting the **Performance** or **Reliability** and **Performance Monitor** from the **Administrative Tools** menu.

This is how the screen will pop up:

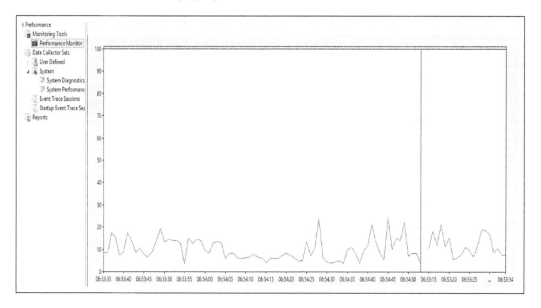

In Perfmon you can configure the performance counters you want to monitor like: physical disk, memory, process, CPU, and network.

Following is the list of the performance counters usually monitored.

- **Server analysis**:
    - PhysicalDisk / % Idle TimePhysicalDisk / Avg. Disk sec/read
    - PhysicalDisk / Avg. Disk sec/write
    - PhysicalDisk / Current Disk Queue Length
    - Memory / Available Mbytes
    - Memory / Pages/sec
    - Memory / Cache Bytes

- **Database analysis**:
    - ° Available MBytes
    - ° % Usage
    - ° Avg. Disk sec/Read– Avg. Disk sec/Write
    - ° Processor Queue Length
    - ° Disk Reads/sec
    - ° Disk Writes/sec
    - ° % Processor Time
    - ° General Statistics – User Connections
    - ° Memory Manager – Memory Grants Pending
    - ° Batch Requests/sec
    - ° Compilations/sec
    - ° Recompilations/sec

- **Some of the common performance bottlenecks are**:
    - ° **Buffer overflow**: This is a bottleneck where a process or a program writing to a buffer exceeds buffer memory and writes to other memory locations.
    - ° **Configuration parameters tuning**: These are the parameters which are configured in the wrong manner, for example Max connections, Flow limit, and so on.
    - ° **Memory Leakage**: This is a bottleneck where a process keeps on holding memory after use, even after the process or program has stopped running.

Let's take a look at SAR and KSAR reporting features:

- **System Activity Report (SAR)**: SAR is a command line utility used to monitor Linux based systems you can monitor most of the performance counters using it. The data collected can further be analyzed to tune the application and increase performance of the application under test. The data presented by SAR reporting is in numerical format and doesn't have an interactive UI also, in case of monitoring multiple systems, each system will require a SAR instance to be run.

- **KSystem Activity Report (KSAR)**: KSAR is the next version of SAR unlike SAR it has to download from SourceForge. It can work in a client server architecture where you are not required to install KSAR on every system you want to monitor. It also has a very interactive UI which can be used to view data in a better form helping you to analyze the performance results faster.

We have now studied how to monitor server-side resources for analysis purposes during a load test.

SoapUI and LoadUI Integration

In this topic we will see how we can integrate **SoapUI** and **LoadUI** together.

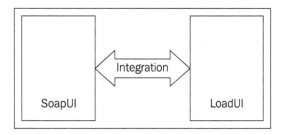

SoapUI can be integrated with LoadUI for any advance performance testing need.

LoadUI has a SoapUI runner which helps in integration and any SoapUI project can then be directly imported and run in LoadUI.

This feature of LaodUI even makes it possible to import functional tests from SoapUI and convert them directly to LOAD test.

Let's see how it works.

Pre-requisites

SoapUI functional Testing project is ready and LoadUI is installed on the machine.

1. Launch LoadUI and verify that the following window pops up:

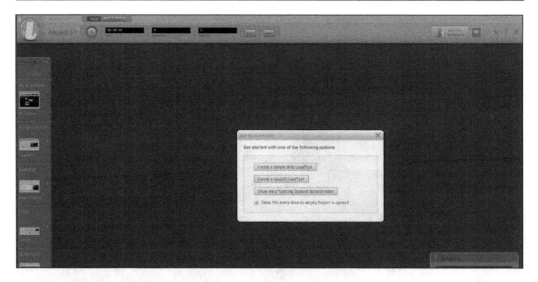

2. Select the **Project Name**:

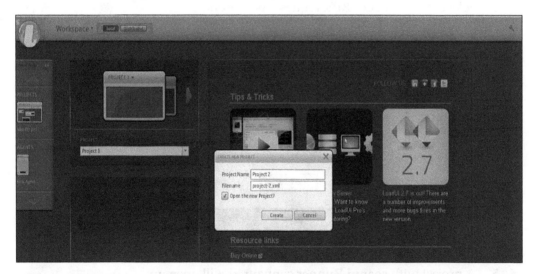

3. Select the option **Create a SoapUI LoadTest**:

4. Select the number of RPS, requests per second:

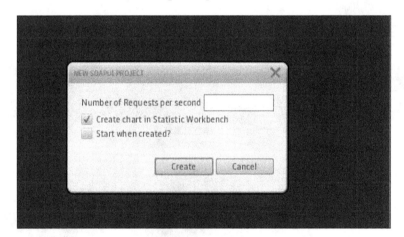

5. A project with **soapui Runner** configured will open up:

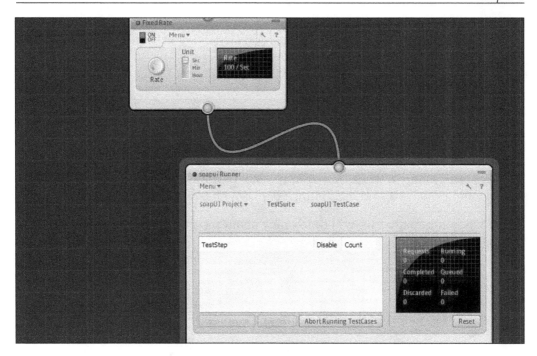

Here you see a **soapui Runner** configured, alternatively you can also pick your Runner from the **Runners** tab displayed on the right-hand side of the screen.

6. Upload the SoapUI project:

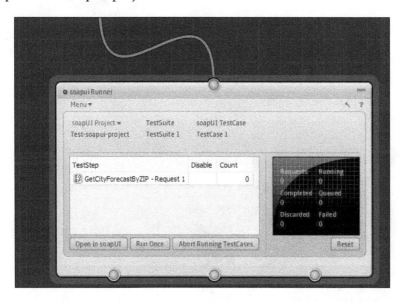

We have now uploaded the SoapUI project and now we can run any performance test in LoadUI for the functional test project created in SoapUI.

This is how we integrate SoapUI with LoadUI!

Summary

So now we have seen how to performance test SOA architecture by generating load on web services. At the end of the chapter, the reader will know the need for Performance testing in the SOA world, types of performance testing, performance test planning, analysis, and integrating SoapUI with LoadUI.

In the following chapter we will be learning about security testing of services in a detailed manner.

4
Security Testing in Detail

In *Chapter 1, Introduction to SOA Testing,* we learnt how to configure SoapUI to test the services from a security perspective. In this chapter we will cover the following topics in detail:

- Security testing in SOA world
- Generating security attacks and analyzing any vulnerabilities
- A real-time example of security testing in Web services

Security testing in SOA world

Service-oriented architecture, as the name implies, is a collection of loosely coupled services which can be over the same or different network. These services talk to multiple databases and share lots of critical information within the organizational services as well as third-parties. The sharing of complex information across multiple WAN and multiple third-party services across enterprises raises concerns for the stakeholders.

Let's have a look at few of the attack types:

- **SQL injection**: The purpose of this attack is to gain access to the database or to get an inappropriate response when we pass SQL fragments in the request parameters.
- **XPath injection**: The purpose of this attack type is to extract information from an XML database.

- **XML bomb**: The purpose of this attack is to result in denial of service for an application. This attacks works by overloading the XML parser recursively by using the entities defined in the DTD.
- **Cross-site scripting attack**: This is a very powerful attack if used in the right combination, this attack targets the user using the application and is capable of transferring the user to unknown locations on the Web, or steal a user's password by capturing keyboard inputs.

As you can see SOA applications are very vulnerable, which raises a need to security test SOA architecture.

SmartBear SoapUI provides you with a set of readymade features and functionalities to test your web services for the following vulnerabilities:

- SQL injection:
- XPath injection
- Fuzzing scan
- Invalid types
- Boundary scans
- Malformed XML
- XML bomb
- Malicious attachment
- CSS attack
- Custom scan

The preceding scan helps to check for any vulnerability that exists in the service and helps us identify security threats more easily.

SoapUI also provides us with an option to custom scan, where you can create your own security test with the help of Groovy or JavaScript.

In the following screenshot you can see an option to **Security Tests** just below **Load Tests** in SoapUI:

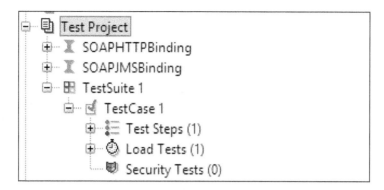

Let's see how we configure a security test in SoapUI:

1. To add a test, right-click on **Security Tests** and select **New SecurityTest**:

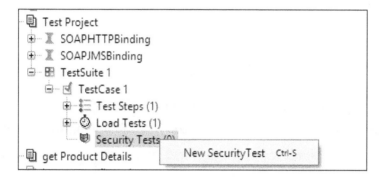

2. Now select **New SecurityTest** and verify that a popup asking the name of the security test opens:

3. Select the name of the security test and click on **OK**.

4. After that you will have a security test configuration window open on the screen; for the Service operation of your test case, in cases where there are multiple operations in the same test case, you can configure for multiple operations in a single security test as well.

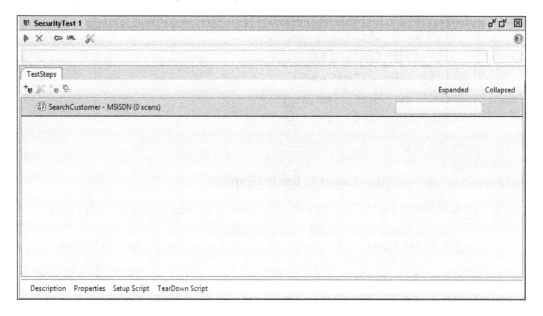

5. For this pane you can select and configure scans on your service operations.

6. To add a scan click on the selected icon in the following screenshot:

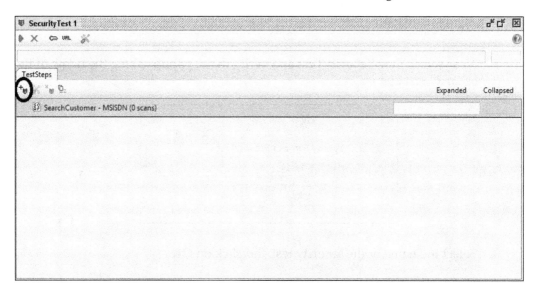

7. After selecting the icon you can now select the scan you want to generate on your operation:

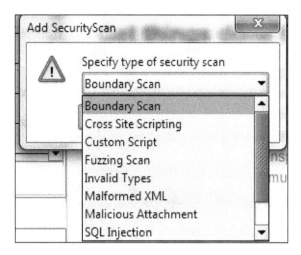

8. After that you can configure your scan for the relevant parameter by configuring the XPath of the parameter in the request. Once you select the test and click on the **OK** button you will be routed to the following screen:

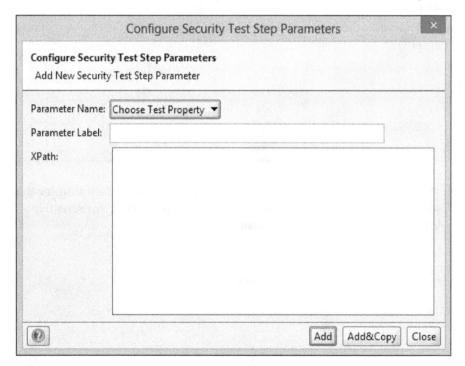

Once you are done with entering the details, you can then add the test with the **Add** button. Once you add the test you can leave the window by clicking on the **Close** button.

9. After that you can select **Assertions** and **Strategy** from the options:

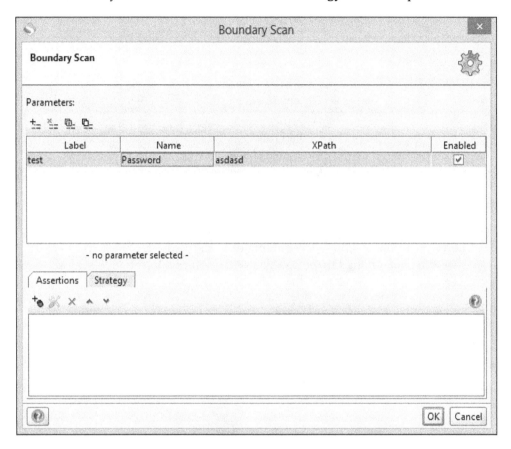

10. You are now ready to run your security test with boundary scan for the search service method and we will be testing the service for sensitive information exposure in response.

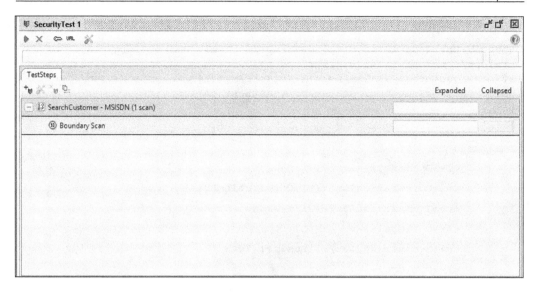

A real time example of security testing in web services

Now let's take a real time example of security testing a web service to be tested: the authentication service.

Web service functionality: The authentication service takes as input, username and password and validates whether the credentials are correct or not.

The test to be configured for this service:

- SQL injection
- XPath injection
- Boundary values scan

Why should we use these? Why the preceding scans only?

Well as we can see, the service is an authentication service and takes as input, username and password. When an attacker attacks this service, it will test techniques to gain unauthorized access to the systems, therefore we use the following attack types to test the service:

- SQL injection
- XPath injection
- Boundary value scans.

Request of the service:

```
<soapenv:Envelope xmlns:soapenv="http://schemas.xmlsoap.org/soap/
envelope/" xmlns:v1="http://xyz/xsd/resource/common/commondefinitions/
msf/messagecontext/v1" xmlns:v11="http://xyz/xsd/interface/user/
useraccount/useraccountmanagement/mcauthentication/v1">
    <soapenv:Header>
        <v1:MessageContext TimeToLive="?" messageID="?" messageType="?"
timestamp="?">
            <!--Optional:-->
            <v1:CorrelationID>?</v1:CorrelationID>
            <v1:TransactionID>?</v1:TransactionID>
            <!--Optional:-->
            <v1:BusinessKey>?</v1:BusinessKey>
            <!--Optional:-->
            <v1:ApplicationID>?</v1:ApplicationID>
            <!--Optional:-->
            <v1:UserID>?</v1:UserID>
            <!--Optional:-->
            <v1:ServiceInstanceID>?</v1:ServiceInstanceID>
            <!--Optional:-->
            <v1:SourceProcess>?</v1:SourceProcess>
        </v1:MessageContext>
    </soapenv:Header>
    <soapenv:Body>
        <v11:AuthenticateRequest>
            <v11:username>Pranai</v11:username>
            <v11:password>Nandan</v11:password>
            <!--You may enter ANY elements at this point-->
        </v11:AuthenticateRequest>
    </soapenv:Body>
</soapenv:Envelope>
```

We will now see how we are going to configure the test with a series of screenshots, starting with the one shown following:

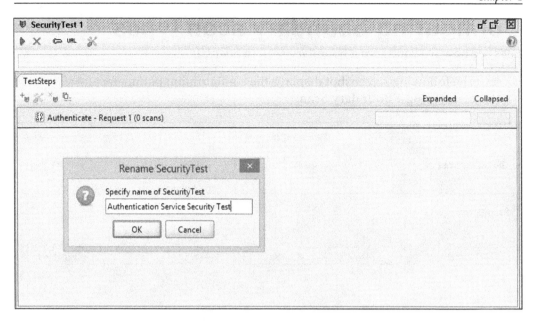

Now, to add scans we need to to add **SecurityScan** as shown in the following figure:

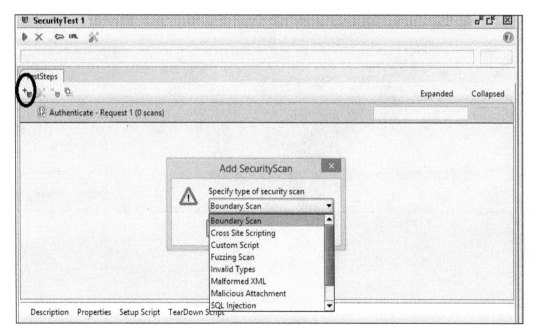

Configuring boundary scan types

Let's see how we configure a boundary scan in SoapUI:

1. The following screenshot displays the configuration parameters for configuring a **Boundary Scan**:

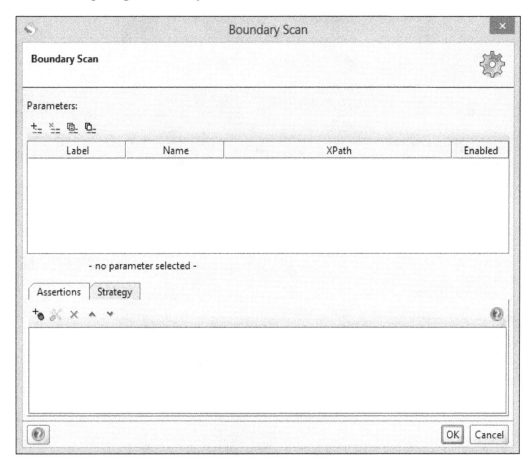

2. In the preceding screenshot, click on the **+** button in the top right of the left hand side of the window. This will further open a pop-up dialog box for further configuration.

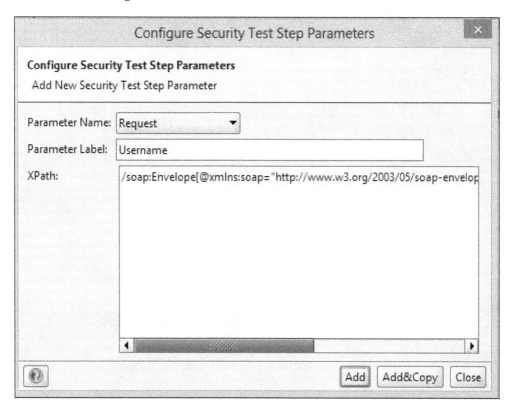

3. In the preceding screenshot we can see that we have configured three values:
   - **Parameter Name**: Target parameter **Request**
   - **Parameter label**: Relevant name of the parameter of the request
   - **XPath**: XPath of the parameter

4. After configuring this, click on the **Add** button and this will add the attack.

5. Similarly, we configure another parameter; **Password**.

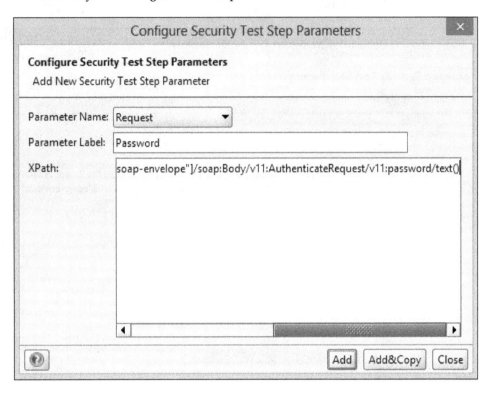

6. Now we have configured a **Boundary Scan** for authentication service:

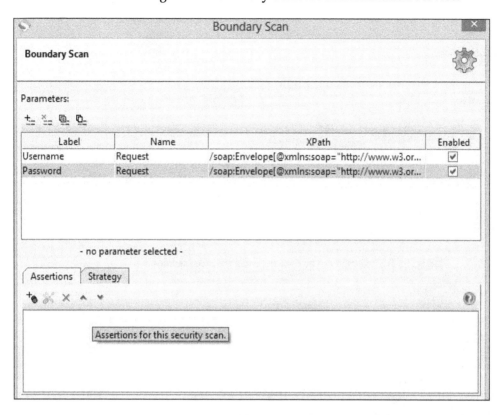

7. Similarly we configure a SQL injection test:

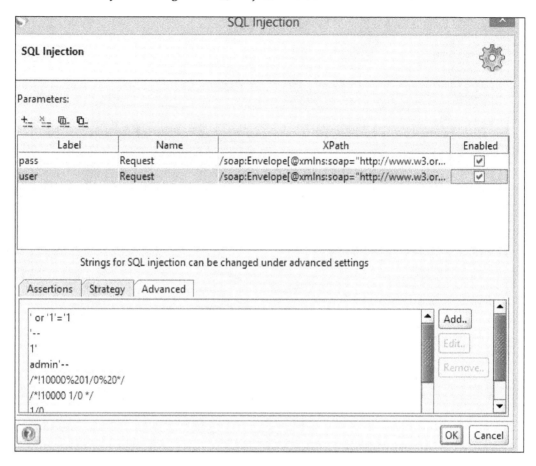

 Note: We can also configure and add SQL injection strings using the **Advanced** tab, as shown in the preceding screenshot.

8. The steps to configure the third scan, which is XPath injection, are the same:

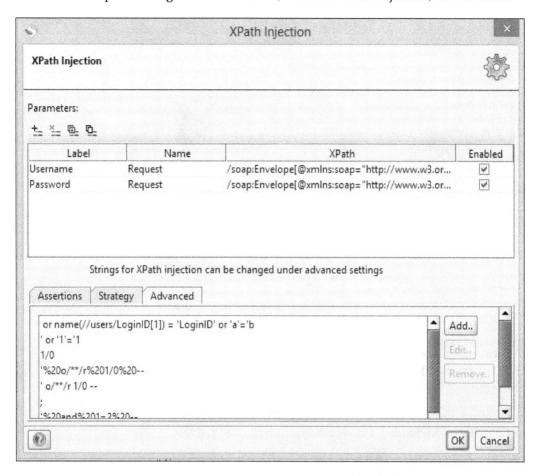

Note: You can always add any other strings using the **Advanced** tab as shown in the previous screenshot.

9. Now we are done configuring request for our authentication service:

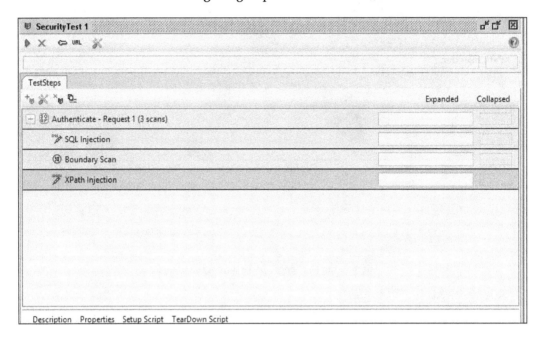

After we have configured the test, it's now time to run the test which is done by clicking on the **Play** button on the top navigation bar on the left hand side of the window.

But before doing that please add a **Security Assertion** for **Sensitive information Exposure**.

The criteria; how we validate whether an assertion is passed or not, is defined by the tokens which are to be verified and can be increased and decreased as per your requirement. Please have a look at the following image for more details. These tokens can be added from the Assertion window - they already have a repository of tokens which can be viewed in the **Preferences** option of SoapUI in the **Global Sensitive Information Tokens** tab.

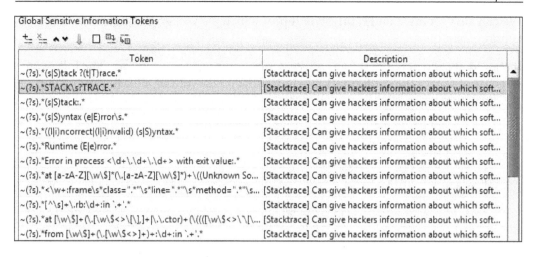

Then we run the test:

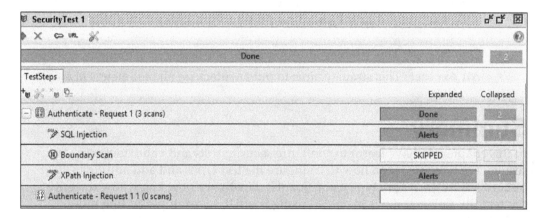

To further dig into the details you can use the logs which are available at the bottom of the screen:

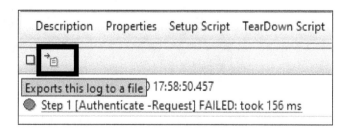

We can also generate an HTML style report which we will go through in the coming chapters.

It should also be noted that you can strategize your test for each scan. The following screenshot shows the configuration window. You may add or alter the strings for SQL injection here.

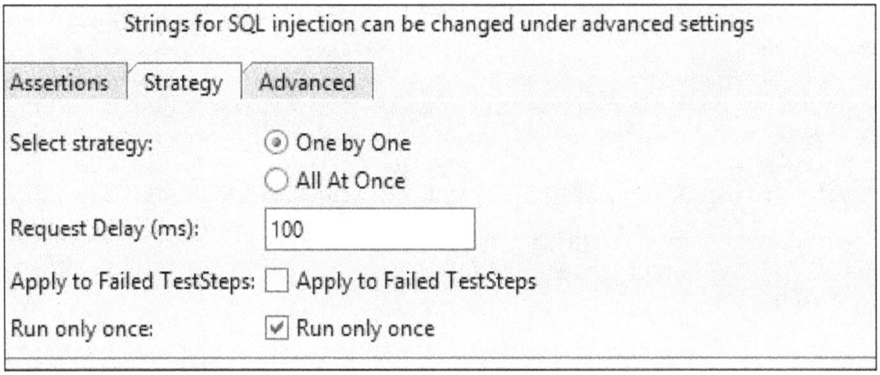

```
        Strings for SQL injection can be changed under advanced settings

 Assertions    Strategy    Advanced

 Select strategy:          ⦿ One by One
                           ○ All At Once

 Request Delay (ms):       100

 Apply to Failed TestSteps: ☐ Apply to Failed TestSteps

 Run only once:            ☑ Run only once
```

- **One by One**: This strategy aims to put the attack on one parameter at a time
- **All At Once**: This strategy aims to put an attack on all parameters at a time

Summary

In this chapter we have learnt to configure security tests and validate the results. We have also seen how to configure the test types and add additional test criteria for each scan type using SoapUI. Finally we now know how to verify the security vulnerabilities in an API using SoapUI, for example adding more SQL injections values.

In the coming chapter we will take a deep look at functional test automation.

5

Test Automation in SOA World

Test automation has evolved in SOA world, in the past years, giving birth to a number of tools practices and standards. But without the right approach to automate, we can't achieve the desired returns, and some of the basic pointers should be kept in mind when planning test automation of SOA applications.

- **Manual testing cannot be replaced with automation testing**: This is the most common mistake people make; a new feature has to be manually tested and when stable it can be automated, Test automation is traditionally for regression testing not a test replacement.

- **Automation testing in SOA has different levels**: Automation testing has different levels like unit level, system level and end-to-end level. Based on the scope and requirements in SOA testing, we first automate the smoke or component test, then the integration test, and finally the end-to-end regression test or orchestration test.

- **An SOA automation test team needs business and technical architecture knowledge to automate scenarios**. This is usually very important, since better understanding of the business and the architecture for the automation tester would provide quality automation suites.

- **Access to the database and repositories are required:** When automation testing SOA architecture, we would need access to the repositories and the system, to which the user doesn't usually have access, since we would need to capture the data from different repositories and validate the results.

- **Any third-party systems should be stubbed or should be accessible:** Any third-party system should either be stubbed with the relevant scenario dynamically, or we should have access to the third-party system.

Test automation ROI

Let's talk about the ROI of test automation:

- Traceability:
    - ° Results from every run captured and stored to be compared in the future

- Repeatability:
    - ° Ability to repeat test cases P1

- Predictability:
    - ° Helps to improve confidence in the product delivered to the business
    - ° Raises quality as each test or selected tests have to be successful

- Time and cost savings:
    - ° Enables broader coverage of test cases/scenarios
    - ° Takes less time than manual

Deliverables to client:

- Documented business flows
- A test plan
- Reusable business automation scripts with minimum maintenance cost
- Complete test process
- Integration of test management tool with automation scripts
- Detailed health analysis of the system

Test automation using SoapUI

A test automation framework is usually comprised of the following:

- **Test drivers**: A test driver is usually the mechanism through which the test is executed
- **Assertion/validations**: Assertions to validate if the test passed or failed
- **Report generating tools**: Report generation to get the test results
- **Clean-up script**: To clear all data generated for test
- **E-mail notification**: E-mail notification of test results

Types of test automation framework

Keyword driven: A keyword driven framework is a collection of keywords, which are maintained in an Excel sheet, and functions are called based on the keyword to complete an end-to-end flow.

Major components of a keyword-driven framework:

- **Excel sheet to store the keywords**: Where you store your keyword with respect to your test cases and terminology selected by you

- **Function library**: Functions that you create which should be tied up with the keywords

- **Data sheets**: Data sheets contacting data

- **Test script or driver script**: Test script and driver script to run the test suites

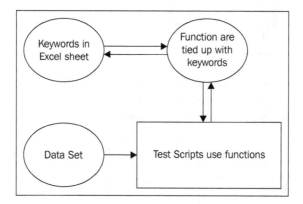

Data-driven framework: As the name suggests, data-driven frameworks are driven by data itself, in the form of hardcoded values within the code, or from an external data source Excel, or notepad. The major drawback of data-driven frameworks is that when the environment changes the scripts may break because of the change in data.

However, it's a rapidly implemented framework, which can be maintained with ease, and could be successful if skilled resources are used to maintain the data for each environment change or revision.

Example of a data-driven framework is show following:

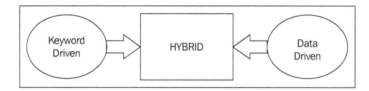

Hybrid framework: This framework uses the best of both of the preceding frameworks. This is the most successful framework, which is used for real time implementation, and is less prone to failures.

We also should focus on our scope before we implement any type of framework.

Scripting types

Linear and modular scripting types are explained following:

- **Linear scripting**: Linear scripting is when we don't implement function-related architecture and directly start scripting without creating any functions. This type of scripting makes it easy to write scripts and could be considered for small scale automation.

- **Modular scripting**: This type of scripting is a function-based scripting where we make use of functions and driver script to achieve desired results. This type of scripting is suitable for large-scale automation.

Now let's have a look at SoapUI open source and SoapUI Pro capabilities for framework creation:

Features	SoapUI	SoapUI Pro
Data source or data read	No [Script required]	Yes
Database connection	No [Script required]	Yes
Reporting	No [Script required]	Yes
E-mail functionality	No [Script required]	Yes with a plugin
Assertions	Yes	Yes
Library extension	Yes	Yes
Dynamic environment switching	No	Yes

Now, as we can see that SoapUI open source has limited functionality available to help us create an automation framework, we would need to create a few utilities ourselves.

Utilities for a test automation framework

Let's start creating a customized script for data source implementation

So what do we need?

- An open source library to help us read from Microsoft Excel
- Documentation of the library to write code

Options available:

- JExcel
- Apache POI

Let's see how to write the script using JExcel.

In SoapUI we have an external (ext) folder where we can place any external library and utilize it in our Groovy script.

This folder is very useful in integrating any tools or external libraries with SoapUI.

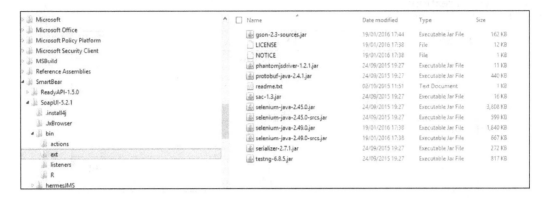

So our first step is to download JExcel, from the following link:

Download link: `https://sourceforge.net/projects/jexcelapi/files/jexcelapi/2.6.12/`

Download the JAR file and place it in the `ext` folder of SoapUI.

Once that is done you are set to write code in Groovy to use JExcel.

For any information on the method and details of the library you can refer to the documentation and the release note of the version you download

Documentation link: `http://www.andykhan.com/jexcelapi/tutorial.html`

Just for information, this library can also be used to perform many other functions with Excel, and can help create a bridge between SoapUI and Excel sheets for the export and import of data.

Ok, so let's start writing some code.

Groovy script for reading data from an Excel sheet

Following is the Groovy script for reading data:

```
import com.eviware.soapui.model.*
import com.eviware.soapui.model.testsuite.Assertable
import com.eviware.soapui.support.XmlHolder
import java.io.File;
import java.util.*;
import jxl.write.*
import jxl.*
def regLogger =
  org.apache.log4j.Logger.getLogger("RegressionTestLoger");
def groovyUtils = new com.eviware.soapui.support.GroovyUtils(
  context )
def properties = new java.util.Properties();
//context.expand('${Properties#propertyname}')
def s2
def s3=(testRunner.testCase.getPropertyValue("RUN"))
regLogger.info(s3);
if (s3 != '1' && s3 != '2' && s3 != '3')
{
  testRunner.testCase.setPropertyValue("RUN", '1' );
  s3=(testRunner.testCase.getPropertyValue("RUN"));


}


Workbook workbook = Workbook.getWorkbook(new
  File("D:\\myfile.xls"))
for (count in 1..< 11)  // This is from row1 to row 11 based on
  the number of properties that you have in the excel sheet in
  this case the values were 10
  {
    Sheet sheet = workbook.getSheet(1)
    Cell a1 = sheet.getCell(0,count) // getCell(row,column) —
    place some values in myfile.xls
```

```
        Cell b2 = sheet.getCell(s3.toInteger(),count)   // values will
            be acessed using a1, b2 & c3 Cell.
        String  s1 = a1.getContents();
        s2 = b2.getContents();
        testRunner.testCase.setPropertyValue(s1,s2);
    }
    workbook.close()
```

Summary of the script

This script serves two objectives:

- Imports the data from the Excel sheet to the properties of SoapUI
- Verifies that the tests are uniquely on each data set

Note that the script utilizes test runner for writing the properties into SoapUI **Properties**:

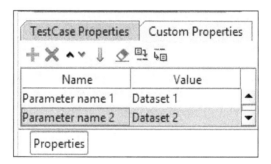

The properties of SOAP can be accessed in SoapUI using `testRunner.testCase.getPropertyValue ("Name of the property"))`.

Let's assume that there were three data sets for each parameter, and you want the test to run uniquely on each data set.

The following screenshot shows an example of an Excel spreadsheet that is suitable for the preceding example:

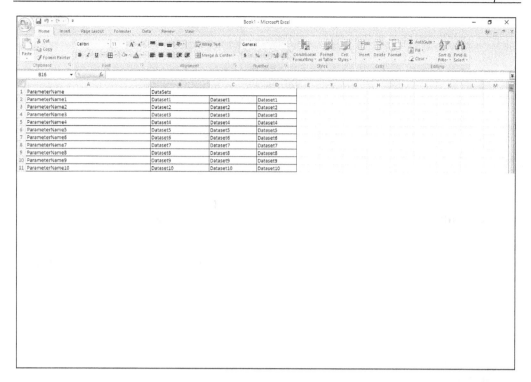

Now, if we look at the second objective, how do we make sure which data set to pick on which run? For that, we need to place a sample script at the last step of the test case, which keeps track of the test run, and updates the value of the property run in the preceding script.

You can also see in the following code how the value is reset to 1:

```
if (s3 != '1' && s3 != '2' && s3 != '3'){  // S3 means the value of
the excel sheet column from where the data values of request are taken
from
testRunner.testCase.setPropertyValue("RUN", '1' );
s3=(testRunner.testCase.getPropertyValue("RUN"));
```

So following is the script that keeps tracks of the run, and can be compared to the data loop functionality in SoapUI Pro:

```
import com.eviware.soapui.support.XmlHolder
def groovyUtils = new com.eviware.soapui.support.GroovyUtils( context
)
Run1 = (testRunner.testCase.getPropertyValue("RUN")).toLong()+1;
  testRunner.testCase.setPropertyValue("RUN",Run1.toString ());
```

The previous script updates the value of the run by 1, so the value picked up is correct, and the test case is run on a unique value each time.

> **Note**: The preceding values are written with respect to the three datasets that are to be imported. The logic can be enhanced as per requirement.
>
> For example, we have three data sets for the request, so the preceding script makes sure that if the value of the run is one, then next time the request runs on the second data set and then the third and finally sets the value to 0.

The JXL utility can be used to create an Excel report that maintains expected results and so on.

We can also use Notepad also for maintaining test data, but Excel is a better solution.

Database connection – why is it required?

We need to interact with databases based on several needs, for example:

- Retrieving a value for orchestration automation where a request generates a unique ID that needs to be passed in the request.
- Storing a value for reporting or auditability purpose.
- Validating a value from the database to the expected value.

We need to use different database drivers for different databases:

Oracle:

- **Name:** OJDBC7.jar
- **Download link:** http://www.oracle.com/technetwork/database/features/jdbc/default-2280470.html

SQL Server:

- **Name:** JDBC drivers
- **Download link:** https://www.microsoft.com/en-us/download/details.aspx?displaylang=en&id=11774

Please note that these driver need to be place in the LIB and ext folders of SoapUI

 Sometimes SoapUI has bugs based on the version you are using, so it's good practice to keep these in both places

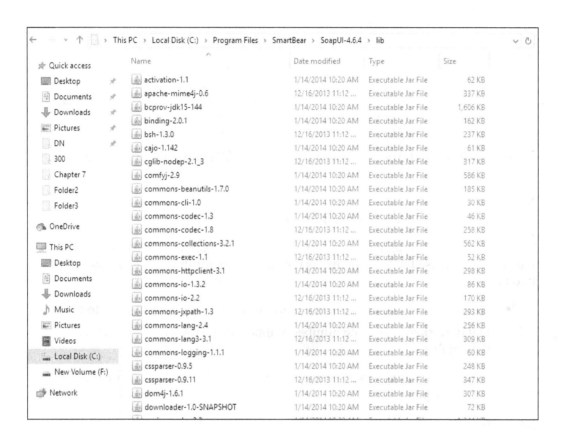

Now let's have look at the following example to connect to an Oracle database:

```groovy
import groovy.sql.Sql;
def regLogger =
  org.apache.log4j.Logger.getLogger("RegressionTestLoger");
def GUID;
def delayStep =
  testRunner.testCase.testSuite.getPropertyValue("delayStep")
def tryCount =
  testRunner.testCase.testSuite.getPropertyValue("delayRetries")
```

```
int x = 1
int y = 0
while ( x <= Integer.parseInt(tryCount) & y != 1  & y != 2 )

{
   println "Delaying " +  Integer.parseInt(delayStep)* 0.001 + "
   seconds."
   Thread.sleep(Integer.parseInt(delayStep))
   def sql =
   groovy.sql.Sql.newInstance
   ("jdbc:oracle:thin:@10.252.168.219:1521:PSYMQA4","CWDEV4SL",
   "CWDEV4SL", "oracle.jdbc.driver.OracleDriver")
   row = sql.firstRow ("select ordstatus, ordtype, GUID, errorcode,
   errorsource, errortext from com_header where accountnumber= "  +
   account +  "order by cwordercreationdate desc")
```

To use a different database, use the appropriate JDBC connection string; please see the documentation for that specific database.

Now, as you can see in the script, we have connected to the database with the connection string and are able to retrieve data from the database.

There is one catch, though, we have to put a retry mechanism in to connect to the database in case the first attempt is not successful; for that we have placed two parameters:

- **Delay count**: This is for a pause between each attempt to connect to database
- **Delay retries**: This is the number of times the script will try to connect to the database

To refer to the logic please refer to the three lines of following code, which are from the preceding script:

[Snippet]

```
while ( x <= Integer.parseInt(tryCount) & y != 1  & y != 2 ){
   println "Delaying " +  Integer.parseInt(delayStep)* 0.001 + "
   seconds."
   Thread.sleep(Integer.parseInt(delayStep))
}
```

For multiple selections from the database you can use the following snippet:

```
sql.eachRow('select * from  tablename where name='Pranai'
```

You may also try to insert and update the tables by using the following statements:

```
def params = [10, 'Name', 'Age']
 sql.execute 'insert into PROJECT (id, name, Age) values (?, ?, ?)',
params
Updating the values of a table

 def newname = 'Nandan'
 def project = 'Testing'
 sql.executeUpdate "update PROJECT set Name=$newname where
name=$project"
```

Now lets consider the need to validate a value from the database to the expected values; in this case we would need to extend the script.

Validation using values retrieved from the database:

```
import groovy.sql.Sql;
def regLogger =
   org.apache.log4j.Logger.getLogger("RegressionTestLoger");
def GUID;
def delayStep =
   testRunner.testCase.testSuite.getPropertyValue("delayStep")
def tryCount =
   testRunner.testCase.testSuite.getPropertyValue("delayRetries")
def account =
   testRunner.testCase.getPropertyValue("imsComboAcct2")
int x = 1
int y = 0
while ( x <= Integer.parseInt(tryCount) & y != 1  & y != 2 )
{
   println "Delaying " +  Integer.parseInt(delayStep)* 0.001 + "
   seconds."

  Thread.sleep(Integer.parseInt(delayStep))

  def sql =
groovy.sql.Sql.newInstance("jdbc:oracle:thin:@10.252.168.219:1521:PSYM
QA4","CWDEV4SL", "CWDEV4SL", "oracle.jdbc.driver.OracleDriver")
  row = sql.firstRow ("select ordstatus, ordtype, GUID, errorcode,
errorsource, errortext from com_header where accountnumber= "  +
account +  "order by cwordercreationdate desc")

  if (row.ordstatus == "COM" ) { y = 1 }
  w=5
   GUID=row.GUID
```

```
        testRunner.testCase.setPropertyValue("GUID1",GUID.toString ());
        testRunner.testCase.setPropertyValue("pranai",w.toString ());

    if (row.ordstatus == "ERR" )    { y = 2 }
    x++
    }

    if  (row.ordstatus == "COM" )
    {
        return (" Passed account# =" + account + " in pending pre-
        provisioning completed in : " +
        x * Integer.parseInt(delayStep) * 0.001 + " sec"  )
        testRunner.testCase.setPropertyValue("checkorder","Passed");

    }

    else

    {
        regLogger.info("*FAILED Acct: " + account + " , Case: " +
        testRunner.testCase.name);
        assert false: "error" + "account#" + account + " status=" +
        row.ordstatus + " source= " +
        row.errorsource + " text=" +  row.errortext + " delay=" + x *
        Integer.parseInt(delayStep) * 0.001 + " sec"
        testRunner.testCase.setPropertyValue("checkorder","Failed");
    }
```

Description of the script:

About the scenario: We need to verify the order status in the database and then mark the test case passed or failed based on it.

`if (row.ordstatus == "ERR"` which means the account is in error state and hence the test case should fail.

Or:

`if (row.ordstatus == "COM"` which means that the account is provisioned and the test case is passed.

We have used assert for validations in the script.

We may also, at certain points, need to validate the number of rows for particular search criteria, and for that the following code might be useful:

```
    def rows = sql.rows("select * from PROJECT where name like 'Pranai%'")
    assert rows.size() == 2
```

So, let's move to our third asset in test automation **reporting**.

Test automation report

As we have seen in the comparison table, the open source version doesn't have the reporting feature. Well it's not true that SoapUI has limited reporting in text format. Let's have a look at it:

1. Launch test runner:

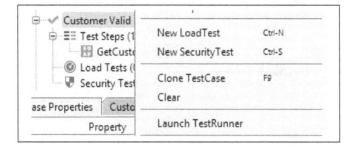

2. Configure the values in the pop up window:

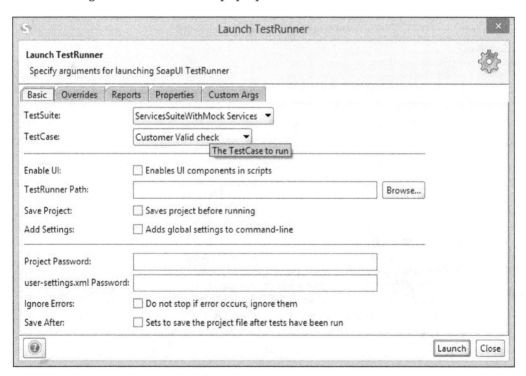

3. Click on the **Launch** button:

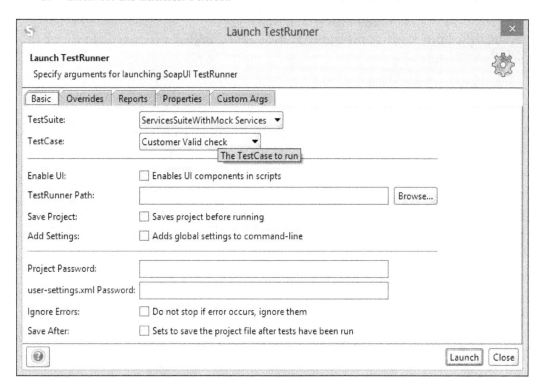

4. Verifies the test starts running:

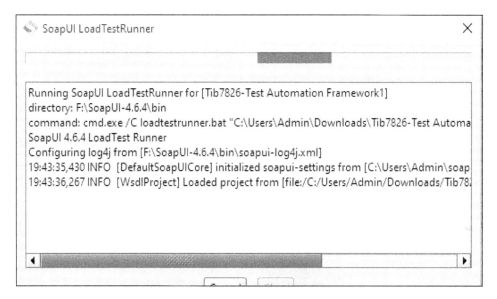

5. Go to the folder that was specified as the destination for reports to be generated:

As you can see in the preceding screenshot, two files are generated in the folder. The text file is one from which report files are generated, whereas the XML file contains the raw results.

Let's have a look at the report:

```
Status: OK
Time Taken: 2384
Size: 1181
Timestamp: Sat Feb 20 12:01:53 GMT 2016
Test Step: GetCustomerValidationRules - Request 1


---------------- Messages ----------------------------

---------------- Properties ----------------------------
Encoding: UTF-8
Endpoint: http://10.97.119.24:9001/IntegrationServices/Customer/
CustomerAccount/CustomerAccountManagement/CustomerAccount_v1/Service/
CustomerAccount_v1.serviceagent/SOAPHTTP

---------------- Request ----------------------------
Request Headers: Host : 10.97.119.24:9001
Content-Length : 2183
SOAPAction : "SOAPHTTP/GetCustomerValidationRules"
Accept-Encoding : gzip,deflate
User-Agent : Apache-HttpClient/4.1.1 (java 1.5)
Connection : Keep-Alive
Content-Type : text/xml;charset=UTF-8


<soap:Envelope xmlns:soap="http://www.w3.org/2003/05/soap-envelope"
xmlns:v1="http://three.co.uk/xsd/resource/common/commondefinitions/
msf/messagecontext/v1" xmlns:v11="http://www.three.co.uk/xsd/
interface/customer/customeraccount/customeraccountmanagement/
customeraccount/v1" xmlns:v12="http://three.co.uk/xsd/cdm/common/
commondefinitions/udf/v1">
    <soap:Header>
```

```
    <v1:MessageContext TimeToLive="?" messageID="?"
    messageType="REQUEST" timestamp="1999-05-31T13:20:00-05:00">
        <!--Optional:-->
        <v1:CorrelationID>?</v1:CorrelationID>
        <v1:TransactionID>?</v1:TransactionID>
        <!--Optional:-->
        <v1:BusinessKey>?</v1:BusinessKey>
        <!--Optional:-->
        <v1:ApplicationID>?</v1:ApplicationID>
        <!--Optional:-->
        <v1:UserID>?</v1:UserID>
        <!--Optional:-->
        <v1:ServiceInstanceID>?</v1:ServiceInstanceID>
        <!--Optional:-->
        <v1:SourceProcess>?</v1:SourceProcess>
    </v1:MessageContext>
</soap:Header>
<soap:Body>
    <v11:GetCustomerValidationRulesRequest>
        <v11:BAN>9600188008</v11:BAN>
        <v11:salesChannel>Contact_Centre</v11:salesChannel>
        <v11:username>PAYMENTS@peoplesoft.three.co.uk</v11:username>
        <v11:orgID>COM01</v11:orgID>
        <v11:contactType>Account Holder</v11:contactType>
        <v11:userLocation>Call Centre</v11:userLocation>
        <v11:validationReason>Upgrade</v11:validationReason>
        <v11:ValidationFactors>
            <!--Zero or more repetitions:-->
            <v11:ValidationFactor>
                <v11:factorID>MEMORABLE_NAME</v11:factorID>
                <v11:factorType>MEMORABLE_NAME</v11:factorType>
                <!--Optional:-->
                <v11:factorSource>My3</v11:factorSource>
                <v11:FactorDetails>
                    <!--Zero or more repetitions:-->
                </v11:FactorDetails>
                <!--You may enter ANY elements at this point-->
            </v11:ValidationFactor>
        </v11:ValidationFactors>
        <!--You may enter ANY elements at this point-->
    </v11:GetCustomerValidationRulesRequest>
</soap:Body>
</soap:Envelope>
```

```
---------------- Response ------------------------
Response Headers: Date : Sat, 20 Feb 2016 12:01:46 GMT
#status# : HTTP/1.1 500 Internal Server Error
Content-Length : 1181
Connection : close
Content-Type : text/xml;charset=utf-8
Server : Apache-Coyote/1.1


<SOAP-ENV:Envelope xmlns:SOAP-ENV="http://schemas.xmlsoap.org/soap/
envelope/">
   <SOAP-ENV:Body>
      <SOAP-ENV:Fault>
         <faultcode>SOAP-ENV:Server</faultcode>
         <faultstring>This is an operation implementation
           generated fault</faultstring>
         <faultactor/>
         <detail>
             <ns:ExceptionInfo context="" description="Invalid
response code received from service" exceptionCode="ERR-MSF-
COMMON-0040" exceptionID="db25cbd5-9600-442f-a9b1-5546551577b4"
exceptionType="TECHNICAL" ns1:Operation="wsGetPaymentMethodDet
ails" ns1:ResponseCode="" ns1:ResponseMessage="Other Exception
Code" ns1:Service="MSF_PaymentGateway-2_root" severity="FATAL"
timestamp="2016-02-20T17:31:46.517+05:30" transactionID="?-
0174be99-872d-47fa-a832-c255e1707017" xmlns:ns="http://three.
co.uk/xsd/resource/common/commondefinitions/msf/exceptioninfo/
v1" xmlns:ns0="http://schemas.xmlsoap.org/soap/envelope/"
xmlns:ns1="http://three.co.uk/xsd/resource/common/commondefinitions/
msf/exceptioninfoextended/v1" xmlns:xs="http://www.w3.org/2001/
XMLSchema" xmlns:xsi="http://www.w3.org/2001/XMLSchema-instance"/>
         </detail>
      </SOAP-ENV:Fault>
   </SOAP-ENV:Body>
</SOAP-ENV:Envelope>
```

As we can see, we don't get comprehensive information or an impressive format in the report and hence there arises a need for a better report for SoapUI open source.

So let's see how to build up an impressive reporting format for SoapUI Open Source.

We'll start with what we will need:

- Apache Ant
- Java path to be set
- Apache Ant path to be set

The most important thing to consider is that we need admin rights on the machine where we are setting things up.

Ok so let's start:

1. Download Apache Ant.

Download Link: `https://ant.apache.org/bindownload.cgi`

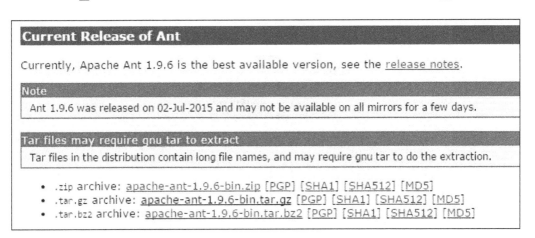

Current Release of Ant

Currently, Apache Ant 1.9.6 is the best available version, see the release notes.

Note

Ant 1.9.6 was released on 02-Jul-2015 and may not be available on all mirrors for a few days.

Tar files may require gnu tar to extract

Tar files in the distribution contain long file names, and may require gnu tar to do the extraction.

- .zip archive: apache-ant-1.9.6-bin.zip [PGP] [SHA1] [SHA512] [MD5]
- .tar.gz archive: apache-ant-1.9.6-bin.tar.gz [PGP] [SHA1] [SHA512] [MD5]
- .tar.bz2 archive: apache-ant-1.9.6-bin.tar.bz2 [PGP] [SHA1] [SHA512] [MD5]

2. Set the path of the Apache Ant in the system:

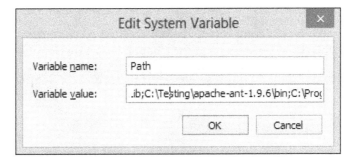

Edit System Variable ✕

Variable name: Path

Variable value: .ib;C:\Testing\apache-ant-1.9.6\bin;C:\Prog

OK   Cancel

Now it's time to download JDK and JRE, if you haven't done so already, and set the Java path.

Next, we have to build the `build.xml` to connect with SoapUI and generate a report:

```
<project name="Project-Dev" default="testreport" basedir=".">
  <target name="soapui">
    <exec dir="." executable="C:/Program Files/SmartBear/
    SoapUI-5.2.1/bin/testrunner.bat">
    <arg line= "-j -f C:/Projects/SoapUI /Production.xml'"/>
    </exec>
  </target>
  <target name = "testreport" depends ="soapui">
    <junitreport todir="C C:/Projects/SoapUI /NewFolder">
    <fileset dir="C:/Users/pnandan/Desktop/Analysis/NewFolder">
      <include name="TEST-TestSuite_1.xml"/>
    </fileset>
    <report todir=" C:/Projects/SoapUI /NewFolder/HTML"
        styledir="C:/Testing/apache-ant-1.9.6/etc"
        format="frames">
    </report>
    </junitreport>
  </target>
</project>
```

Let's go through `build.xml`:

- For the execution of test cases, `build.xml` has set the path to the test runner. Have a look at the following line:

  ```
  [executable="C:/Program Files/SmartBear/SoapUI-5.2.1/bin/
  testrunner.bat"]
  ```

- The path of the project to execute is also provided to run the specific project which may contain a number of test suites:

  ```
  [arg line= "-j -f 'C:/Users/pnandan/Desktop/Analysis/NewFolder'
  C:/Users/pnandan/Desktop/Test/Pranai/Production.xml]
  ```

- The path of eports to be gencrated is given here:

  ```
  [report todir="C:/Users/pnandan/Desktop/Analysis/NewFolder/HTML]
  ```

- The path to the directory of Apache Ant is given here:

  ```
  [Styledir="C:/Testing/apache-ant-1.9.6/etc"]
  ```

- If you see a specific test suite report you can specify the name of it:

  ```
  [include name="TEST-TestSuite_1.xml"]
  ```

Now let's start by executing the test and viewing the report.

Executing the test:

1. Open the command prompt:

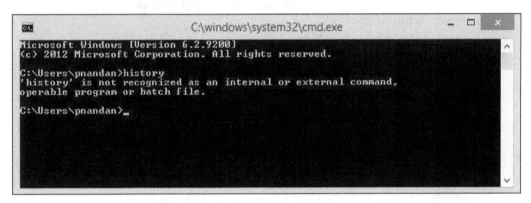

2. Go to the folder containing `build.xml` and type `ant`:

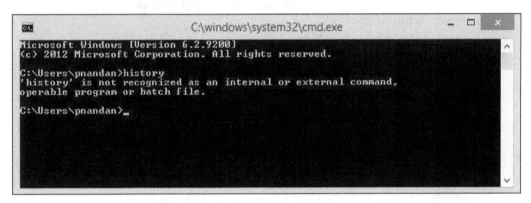

3. Verify that the execution starts:

```
apui:
    [exec] 12:44:40,646 INFO  [SoapUI] Adding [C:\Program Files\SmartBear\SoapU
5.2.1\bin\ext\gson-2.3-sources.jar] to extensions classpath
    [exec] 12:44:40,647 INFO  [SoapUI] Adding [C:\Program Files\SmartBear\SoapU
5.2.1\bin\ext\phantomjsdriver-1.2.1.jar] to extensions classpath
    [exec] 12:44:40,648 INFO  [SoapUI] Adding [C:\Program Files\SmartBear\SoapU
5.2.1\bin\ext\protobuf-java-2.4.1.jar] to extensions classpath
    [exec] 12:44:40,648 INFO  [SoapUI] Adding [C:\Program Files\SmartBear\SoapU
5.2.1\bin\ext\sac-1.3.jar] to extensions classpath
    [exec] 12:44:40,649 INFO  [SoapUI] Adding [C:\Program Files\SmartBear\SoapU
5.2.1\bin\ext\selenium-java-2.45.0-srcs.jar] to extensions classpath
    [exec] 12:44:40,650 INFO  [SoapUI] Adding [C:\Program Files\SmartBear\SoapU
5.2.1\bin\ext\selenium-java-2.45.0.jar] to extensions classpath
    [exec] 12:44:40,650 INFO  [SoapUI] Adding [C:\Program Files\SmartBear\SoapU
5.2.1\bin\ext\selenium-java-2.49.0-srcs.jar] to extensions classpath
    [exec] 12:44:40,650 INFO  [SoapUI] Adding [C:\Program Files\SmartBear\SoapU
5.2.1\bin\ext\selenium-java-2.49.0.jar] to extensions classpath
    [exec] 12:44:40,651 INFO  [SoapUI] Adding [C:\Program Files\SmartBear\SoapU
5.2.1\bin\ext\serializer-2.7.1.jar] to extensions classpath
```

4. When the execution finishes, go to the folder specified in the `build.xml`:

Name	Date modified	Type	Size
Test Project	20/02/2016 12:44	File folder	
allclasses-frame.html	20/02/2016 12:45	Chrome HTML Do...	1 KB
all-tests.html	20/02/2016 12:45	Chrome HTML Do...	4 KB
alltests-errors.html	20/02/2016 12:45	Chrome HTML Do...	1 KB
alltests-fails.html	20/02/2016 12:45	Chrome HTML Do...	3 KB
alltests-skipped.html	20/02/2016 12:45	Chrome HTML Do...	1 KB
index.html	20/02/2016 12:45	Chrome HTML Do...	1 KB
overview-frame.html	20/02/2016 12:45	Chrome HTML Do...	1 KB
✓ overview-summary.html	20/02/2016 12:45	Chrome HTML Do...	2 KB
stylesheet.css	20/02/2016 12:45	Cascading Style S...	1 KB

5. To view the summary, open the file overview-summary.html:

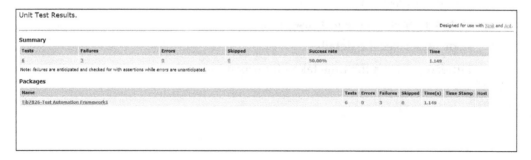

Unit Test Results.

Designed for use with JUnit and Ant.

Summary

Tests	Failures	Errors	Skipped	Success rate	Time
6	3	0	0	50.00%	1.149

Note: *failures* are anticipated and checked for with assertions while *errors* are unanticipated.

Packages

Name	Tests	Errors	Failures	Skipped	Time(s)	Time Stamp	Host
Tib7B26-Test Automation Framework1	6	0	3	0	1.149		

6. Now if you want to see a detailed view, click on the test project hyperlink:

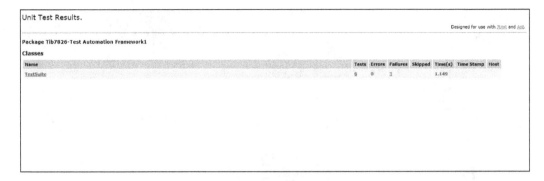

On the previous page, click on the test suite name for which you want to see the detailed analysis. In this case, there is only one test suite to choose from.

Detailed summary report:

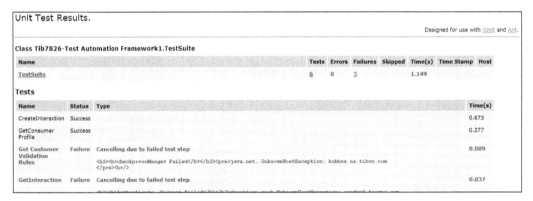

As we now see, we can view the detailed report for the test suites. Let's go by the nomenclature of the reports:

- **Name**: represents the test case name
- **Status**: represents the test case status
- **Type**: describes the details
- **Time**: represents the time taken for execution of the test cases

Note: People might be wondering how the report is generated. If you remember, the SoapUI test runner generates a raw XML file of results. We use that raw result and pass it into a better format.

Here is where you can find the `.xml` file:

Name	Date modified	Type	Size
ExportAsWar	15/01/2016 12:23	File folder	
HTML	25/01/2016 10:47	File folder	
9991200515122400046491.pdf	24/12/2015 07:28	PDF File	29 KB
☑ TESTS-TestSuites.xml	20/02/2016 12:45	XML File	14 KB
TestSuite_1-Create_Interaction-CreateI...	20/02/2016 12:45	Text Document	3 KB
TestSuite_1-Get_Consumer_Profile-Ge...	20/02/2016 12:45	Text Document	2 KB
TestSuite_1-Search_Customer-Search...	20/02/2016 12:45	Text Document	3 KB
TEST-TestSuite_1.xml	20/02/2016 12:45	XML File	14 KB

Now we have two XML files: one specific to a test suite and the other to the project. If your test project has multiple test suites you can pass the `TESTS-TestSuites.xml` in your `build.xml` file.

So now we know how to generate a more structured report in SoapUI, but there is still one challenge to face, which is auditability.

If we need to track the result of the old test runs that were done then we don't have a mechanism yet, since in the current structure the new report data always overwrites the old one.

So, to achieve auditability we have another `build.xml`, extending the previous build.xml, that will provide you a better structure of reports and auditability:

```
<project name="Project-Dev" default="testreport" basedir=".">
  <target name="soapui">
    <tstamp>
      <format property="timestamp" pattern="yyyyMMddHHmmss"/>
    </tstamp>
```

```
    <exec dir="." executable="C:/Program Files/SmartBear/
      SoapUI-5.2.1/bin/testrunner.bat">
    <arg line= "-j -f
    'C:/Users/pnandan/Desktop/Analysis/NewFolder'
    'C:/Users/pnandan/Desktop/Test/Pranai/Production.xml'"/>
    </exec>
  </target>
  <target name = "testreport" depends ="soapui">
    <junitreport todir=
        "C:/Users/pnandan/Desktop/Analysis/NewFolder">
      <fileset dir="C:/Users/pnandan/Desktop/Analysis/NewFolder">
        <include name="TEST-TestSuite_1.xml"/>
      </fileset>
      <report todir=
          "C:/Users/pnandan/Desktop/Analysis/NewFolder/HTML"
          styledir="C:/Testing/apache-ant-1.9.6/etc"
          format="noframes">
      </report>
    </junitreport>
    <move file=
        "C:/Users/pnandan/Desktop/Analysis/NewFolder/HTML/
        junit-noframes.html" tofile=
        "C:/Users/pnandan/Desktop/Analysis/NewFolder/HTML/
        soapUIResults/soapUIResults-${timestamp}.html"/>
  </target>
</project>
```

Now here, in the preceding `build.xml`, we are consolidating the results in a single page and using the timestamp feature to name the report by the timestamp, so that you can trace your test results history. The changes from the previous `build.xml` are highlighted.

So let's have a look at the new structure of the reports and the report itself:

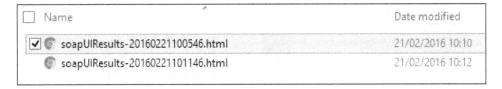

As you can see, the names of the report end with the timestamp by which you can easily recognize the last runs and also compare them as.

Folder structure:

The new folder structure contains the new folder `soapUIResults` that has the new reports format and all the reports of the last runs.

New report:

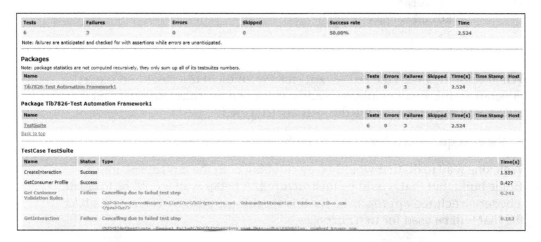

So as you can see, we no longer have a drill down report; a single page tells us about the status of the tests.

E-mail notification:

Well, since now we know how to generate a report, we would like to send automatic notifications to the stakeholders to the e-mail with the reports attached, so let's see how we can achieve that.

For e-mail notification we need to use `Javamail.jar` and place it in the following path: `C:\Testing\apache-ant-1.9.6\lib#`

Now when you have done that, we can proceed with the `build.xml` file:

```
<target description="Generates and send junit test reports"
name="send-report">
  <mail mailhost="your mail host" mailport="your mail host port"
    password="your password" ssl="true" subject="Test build"
    user="your email id">
    <from address="pranainandan08@gmail.com"></from>
    <replyto address="SIT @gmail.com"></replyto>
    <to address="SIT @gmail.com"></to>
    <message>The Test Run has been completed</message>
    <attachments>
      <fileset dir="attachment directory path">
        <include name="**/*.zip"></include>
     </fileset>
    </attachments>
  </mail>
</target>
```

When combined with the `build.xml` for execution of test cases and report generation, this functionality will add a cherry on the cake and send you automated reports each time the tests are triggered.

So the next question is how do we combine them together?

Well, one way to do that would be by clubbing both the `build.xml` into a single build, but that would be unstructured. A better way would be to create a better-structured approach. So for this specific purpose we can create a BAT file that will be used for two purposes:

* To run the `build.xml` for execution and report generation
* To run the `build.xml` for sending the e-mail with the report attached

So here is your batch file to do that:

```
set Script=C:\\SOAP_Test\
   cd %Script%
 call ant -f  Build.xml
set Script=C:\\mfg
  %progdrive%
 cd %Script%


 call ant -f Build.xml


 pause(100000000000000)
```

A deliberate pause is given, so that the message that the e-mail is being delivered is displayed for a while on the screen.

This script can be further enhanced to your requirements.

To run this script you just need to click on it.

	Name	Date modified	Type	Size
☑	Executionofproject.bat	21/02/2016 14:32	Windows Batch File	1 KB

Dynamic environment configuration

We often see situations where we need to frequently target our tests on different environments such as staging, prod, pre prod, and QA.

We have two ways to do it. Let's discuss it:

Strategy 1:

1. Put the environment variable into a spreadsheet
2. Load the environment variable in the properties folder of SoapUI
3. Use a regular expression to parameterize the end point URL

With this first technique configured, you just need to change the environment in the Excel sheet and the test will run on the specific environment.

We have already have seen how to achieve Step1 and 2 (data upload from Excel Groovy script). Now here is an example of how to construct a regular expression to parameterize a test:

Creating a property at project level:

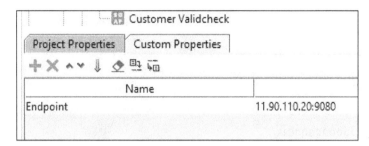

Now once the property is created you can pass a regular expression like this:

${#Project#Endpoint} to the endpoint URL

The endpoint would look like: `http://${#Project#Endpoint}/Test/Test1/services/HTTP`.

This is an effective way of achieving dynamic end point validation.

Strategy 2:

Another way of doing it is through Groovy script. If you want to use Groovy script to do this please find it following:

```
import com.eviware.soapui.model.*
import com.eviware.soapui.model.testsuite.Assertable
import com.eviware.soapui.support.XmlHolder
import java.io.File;
import java.util.*;
import jxl.write.*
import jxl.*
import com.eviware.soapui.support.XmlHolder
import com.eviware.soapui.model.*
import com.eviware.soapui.model.testsuite.Assertable
import com.eviware.soapui.support.XmlHolder
def groovyUtils = new com.eviware.soapui.support.GroovyUtils( context
)
import java.io.File;

def regLogger = org.apache.log4j.Logger.getLogger("RegressionTestLog
er");

def properties = new java.util.Properties();
```

```
def environment = context.expand( '${#TestSuite#Environment}' )
def myEndpoint = environment

//def myEndpoint = "http://10.10.101.1/myApplicationAPI/version2.1/
service.svc"
def project = context.testCase.testSuite.project
 testSuiteList = project.getTestSuites()
 text = "~"
 testSuiteList.each
 {
 testSuite = project.getTestSuiteByName(it.key)
 testCaseList = testSuite.getTestCases()
 log.info " ${text*5} TestSuite :: $testSuite.name"
 testCaseList.each
  {
  testCase = testSuite.getTestCaseByName(it.key)
  log.info " ${text*5} Testcase :: $testCase.name"

  wsdlTestSteps = testCase.getTestStepsOfType( com.eviware.soapui.
impl.wsdl.teststeps.WsdlTestRequestStep.class )
  wsdlTestSteps.each
   {

   it.properties['Endpoint'].value = myEndpoint
   }
  }
 }
 log.info "All the endpoints are now : $Endpoint desired"
```

The preceding scripts works by taking in the endpoint value stored at the test case level as their input and setting the endpoint of all the test cases in the corresponding test suite to the desired end point.

Assertions or validation

We have already discussed this in the previous chapters, so to recap what we have discussed here is a checklist:

- Property content assertions
- Compliance, status and standards
- SLA
- JMS
- Security
- Database assertions (in the current chapter we have seen examples of these)

So the only assertion that's left is script assertion where we need to write scripts to verify certain validations.

Let's take an example:

Example 1: Consider an application where a request once triggered by SoapUI now hits multiple subsystems. You want to validate whether the request you sent hits certain domains at the backend or not, which is stored in the database:-

Here is an example:

```
import groovy.sql.Sql;
import java.util.regex.Matcher;
import java.util.regex.Pattern;
import com.eviware.soapui.model.*
import com.eviware.soapui.model.testsuite.Assertable
import org.junit.Assert.*;
import com.eviware.soapui.support.XmlHolder
import java.io.File; import java.util.*;
def regLogger = org.apache.log4j.Logger.getLogger("RegressionTestLog
er");
def groovyUtils = new com.eviware.soapui.support.GroovyUtils( context
)
def properties = new java.util.Properties();

int x = 1
int y = 0

def sql=groovy.sql.Sql.newInstance("jdbc:oracle:thin:@17.239.192.134:2
296:DAEH","app_eai", "123", "oracle.jdbc.driver.OracleDriver")

def data =sql.rows("SELECT Distinct DOMAIN FROM EH_TRACE_LOG WHERE
EVENT_LOCAL_ID=" + Prop + "")  // Prop is unique Identifier
testRunner.testCase.setPropertyValue("ActualDomainHit",data.
toString());
def Prop =testRunner.testCase.getPropertyValue("MSSIDtobeusedfordb");


def Expected=testRunner.testCase.getPropertyValue("ExpectedDomainHit")
def Actual=testRunner.testCase.getPropertyValue("ActualDomainHit")

assert Actual =~ Expected
```

In this script we are validating whether the backend domains that should be hit by a particular request are hit or not. We are storing the results to the database as an ActualDomainHit and we are comparing it against the expected values

Example 2: Data validation.

We usually want to validate the data in real time with the expected values. To do that, SoapUI provides us with an XPath assertion and an XQuery assertion, but if you want to do it with help of Groovy script, that is possible as well. The following is an example of how to achieve that in real time:

```
import com.eviware.soapui.support.XmlHolder
import com.eviware.soapui.model.*
import com.eviware.soapui.model.testsuite.Assertable
import com.eviware.soapui.support.XmlHolder
import java.io.File;
import java.util.*;
import jxl.write.*
import jxl.*
import com.eviware.soapui.support.XmlHolder
import com.eviware.soapui.model.testsuite.Assertable
import com.eviware.soapui.support.XmlHolder
import java.io.File;
import com.eviware.soapui.support.*;
import java.util.*;
import java.lang.*;
def groovyUtils = new com.eviware.soapui.support.GroovyUtils( context
)
def project = context.testCase.testSuite.project
def holder = groovyUtils.getXmlHolder( "getSROrderData 02#Response" )
holder.namespaces["ProvTypes"] = "http://xml.comcast.com/
provisioning_/types"
holder.namespaces["CSCTypes"] = "http://xml.comcast.com/common/types"
holder.namespaces["ProvServices"] = "http://xml.comcast.com/
provisioning_/services"
def L=testRunner.testCase.getPropertyValue("productIDHSD")
def ProvisionStatus = holder.getNodeValue("//ProvServices:SubmitPro
visioning[1]/ProvServices:ProvisioningReqType[1]/ProvTypes:serviceRe
questCustomerService[1]/ProvTypes:serviceRequestCustomerService[1]/
ProvisionStatus/text()")
def NewOrderStatus =holder.getNodeValue("//ProvServices:SubmitProvi
sioning[1]/ProvServices:ProvisioningReqType[1]/ProvTypes:serviceReq
uestCustomerService[1]/ProvTypes:serviceRequestCustomerService[1]/
InstallStatus[1]/text()")
if (ProvisionStatus==Pass && NewOrderStatus =="SUCCESS!")
{
testRunner.testCase.setPropertyValue("New Install Status
scenario","Passed")
testRunner.testCase.setPropertyValue("scenario",m)
}
```

```
else
{
testRunner.testCase.setPropertyValue("New Install Status
scenario","Failed")
}
```

The previous script is used to validate the response data for two values:

- `ProvisionStatus`
- `NewOrderStatus`

If the status is success for both fields, it signifies that the request was successful and hence we can mark the test case as passed; otherwise we can mark the test case as failed.

Assertions are the most powerful weapon of software automation testers, and we should list down the assertion types before designing any automation framework or planning for automation in the project. This gives you a foresight of things and you can plan as per you needs.

Well this brings us to the end of the test automation framework design utilities section, but before we close it, would like to share some sample script which can be handy while you test automate your applications:

Running a test case using a Groovy script:

```
def testStep = testRunner.testCase.testSteps['Test Step name1']
for (count in 0..< 2)
{
testStep.run( testRunner, context)
}
def testStep1 = testRunner.testCase.testSteps['Test Step name2']

for (count1 in 0..< 2)

{testStep1.run( testRunner, context)

}


def testStep2 = testRunner.testCase.testSteps['Test Step name3']

for (count2 in 0..< 2)

{testStep2.run( testRunner, context)

}
```

Since we are ready with the utilities we can design the test automation framework.

Test automation framework design hybrid

Things required:

- Test cases in an Excel sheet and test case creation in SoapUI
- Data set
- Validations
- Report
- Unique data

Requirement 1: Test cases in an Excel sheet and test case creation

TC_ID	Test case name	Description	Result	Candidate for automation	Automated
TC_01	Order orchestration for a new order	Verify that Successful response is returned when valid data is passed in the request	Pass	Yes	In progress

So now we need to have the name of the test case in the Excel sheet the same as the name of the automated test case in SoapUI

You can do that manually while creating the test case, or you can improvise by writing a Groovy script by accessing the name of the test case by using following code:

Script for creating a test project using Groovy script:

```
import com.eviware.soapui.impl.wsdl.teststeps.registry.
GroovyScriptStepFactory
suite = context.testCase.testSuite.project.addNewTestSuite("TestAutom
ationDemo")
tc = suite.addNewTestCase("Order Orchestration for a New order ")
gs = tc.addTestStep( GroovyScriptStepFactory.GROOVY_TYPE, "ali's
GroovyScript" )
gs.properties["script"].value = 'log.info(\'hello world\')'
context.testCase.testSuite.project.save()
```

This script can further be utilized with the test data import script to automatically create all the test cases in SoapUI. Following are the steps to do that:

1. Import the name of the test cases with the test case ID using the utility of test data import.

2. Loop the script for test case creation for the number of test cases.

This will then create all your dummy test cases in SoapUI.

Requirement 2: Test data

Now let's move to the second most important feature which is test data. We can not only import test data but also any initialization values like database passwords, Endpoint, and important credentials, so we will break this into two categories

• Test initialization data

• Test request data

Both of these should be maintained in an Excel sheet and can be imported using test data import script, however below an example for test initialization script:

```
import com.eviware.soapui.model.*
import com.eviware.soapui.model.testsuite.Assertable
import com.eviware.soapui.support.XmlHolder
import java.io.File;
import java.util.*;
import jxl.write.*
import jxl.*
def regLogger = org.apache.log4j.Logger.getLogger("RegressionTestLog
er");
def groovyUtils = new com.eviware.soapui.support.GroovyUtils( context
)
def properties = new java.util.Properties();


Workbook workbook = Workbook.getWorkbook(new File("D:\\
TestinitializationProperties.xls"))
for (count in 0..< 1)
{
Sheet sheet = workbook.getSheet(1)
Cell a1 = sheet.getCell(0,count)
String  s1 = a1.getContents();
Cell b2 = sheet.getCell(1,count)
String  s7 = b2.getContents();

testRunner.testCase.testSuite.setPropertyValue(s1,s7);
}
```

So now we know how to load the test data and initialization values.

Requirement 3: Validations

Validation script can be created previously if we understand the scope of automation and architecture of the application. Here is an example of how dummy validation scripts can be created:

Do you remember the script that we created for validations? I have just modified it to make it generic

```
def holder = groovyUtils.getXmlHolder( "Name of the step #Response" )
holder.namespaces["namespace1"] = "value1"
holder.namespaces["namespace2"] = "value2"
holder.namespaces["namespace3"] = "value3"
def ProvisionStatus = holder.getNodeValue("Xpath")
def NewOrderStatus =holder.getNodeValue("Xpath"))
if (ProvisionStatus== "expected value" && NewOrderStatus ==" expected
value ")
{
testRunner.testCase.setPropertyValue("New Install Status
scenario","Passed")
testRunner.testCase.setPropertyValue("scenario",m)
}
else
{
testRunner.testCase.setPropertyValue("New Install Status
scenario","Failed")
}
```

So now we see that we can create reusable script for validations.

Requirement 4: Reporting

As we discussed previously, we can always generate the report using the scripts . We have seen in previous sections of this chapter the use of Ant and how to generate reports, so this should now be easy for the readers of this book to create reports for their automation framework.

Requirement 5: Unique data

In certain cases, a situation arises where each time the test request is run we need to send unique data in one or other of the parameters. For this specific purpose you can use the random number generation script and use it for your test data creation:

```
def UniqueID;
def regLogger = org.apache.log4j.Logger.getLogger("RegressionTestLog
er");
try{
synchronized(log)
{
    UniqueID = (testRunner.testCase.testSuite.
getPropertyValue("UniqueID")).toLong()+1000;
    testRunner.testCase.testSuite.setPropertyValue("UniqueID",Unique
ID.toString ());
    testRunner.testCase.setPropertyValue("UniqueID",UniqueID.toString
());
    regLogger.info("* UniqueID: " + UniqueID + " , Case: " +
testRunner.testCase.name);
}
}catch(Exception e){
log.info(Error+e);
}
```

With this we come to the end of creating a test automation framework, which has flavors of keyword, as well as a data-driven framework and hence is a hybrid.

I would recommend that you create these scripts as a SoapUI project and as a master test case so whenever you are required to reuse your script you can just drag and drop it. This will cut your test automation creation time significantly.

The following screenshot that displays how you should configure your reusable test scripts:

> **Note**: The master test suite and test initialization cases are deliberately disabled as we don't want them to run as a part of our real tests.

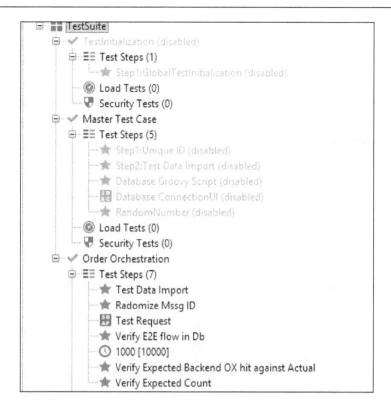

As you can see in the screenshot, we have a master test case and a test initialization test case as reusable scripts, and order orchestration as a real test case where we are reusing the scripts of the master test case and the test initialization.

Since we have now finished creating an end-to-end framework, let's have a look at its advantages:

- **Data-driven testing**: Provides a mechanism to parameterize test data having its data source as an Excel spreadsheet

- **Connecting and querying databases easily**: Provides a mechanism for integration with multiple databases like SQL Server, Oracle, DB2

- **Integration with UI automation tools**: Provides seamless integration with the rich and famous automation tool Selenium to address any multilayer testing needs, or capture and assert UI elements based on different UI technologies like GWT, ExtJS, JavaScript and JSP

- **Auto-configuration of environments/endpoints**: Provides a mechanism to change the endpoint of all the test cases in a test suite with a single click in order to allow switching between multiple environments, for example, QA, staging, and production
- **Dynamic data assertions**: Asserts data based on input data passed
- **Flexibility**: Integrates with third-party systems like Hermes JMS and tools like Selenium and JUnit
- **Reporting**: Provides an enhanced HTML report with the history of reports tracked

And finally to conclude this chapter we come to the summary of it.

Summary

In this chapter we have discussed, in detail, test automation in the SOA world, creating automation frameworks using famous techniques, creating reusable assets for your automation framework, and designing an automation framework.

In the coming chapter we will learn in detail about automating multilayer architecture using Selenium and SoapUI.

6
Multilayer Test Automation Using SoapUI and Selenium

In SOA-world, we have services which are tied up with the frontend. The front end is tied up with the service, which takes care of the business process and orchestration. So in order to validate the end to end flow from UI to service and then to the legacy systems or backend, we will need to test the integration between all the layers and check the connectivity from technical and functional perspectives across applications.

In this chapter we look at the following things:

- Multilayer testing
- Integrating Selenium and SoapUI
- Locators identification for UI
- Automating multilayer test cases using Selenium and SoapUI together

Also when we go ahead testing an end to end flow in an enterprise application we often see that some of the third-party or legacy services are not exposed to us because of security concerns and we have to invoke it through the UI in order to complete the end to end flow.

Let's see an example of business flow - a sample orchestration flow:

1. Service 1.
2. Service 2.
3. Invoke UI, copy the newly generated ID from the UI.

4. Invoke service 3, pass the ID from step 3 to step 4, request.

5. Invoke service 4.

6. Invoke UI, complete, process, submit order.

So as we can see in the preceding example we have four calls that are to be invoked using service and two calls which are invoked using the UI.

So in order to test this flow manually we would need to run services and the UI and check the validation points.

Now how do we automate it? We know that SoapUI isn't capable of UI test automation and other tools, like Selenium or QTP, could invoke a service directly.

The preceding question makes it clear to us that we need a single tool with the capability of the UI as well as service automation.

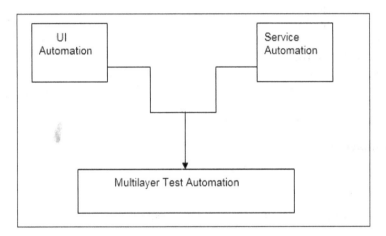

We know that SoapUI is the most used tool for Web services so let's test automation and let's have a look at UI test automation tools.

UI test automation tools

Let's have a look at some of the famous test automation tools:

- **VSTS Ultimate**: **Visual Studio Test System** is a testing tool bundled with Visual Studio Ultimate. There are various add-ons available to support the testing of various types of applications.

- **QTP**: **Quick Test Professional** is a functional testing tool from HP and it supports various applications including the .NET applications with the help of the .NET Extensibility add-on.

- **Selenium**: Selenium is a portable software testing framework for web applications. Selenium provides two versions, the IDE (browser plugin) and the Webdriver. The best and the latest today is Web driver which addresses most of the challenges of the previous versions and enables multibrowser test automation. It also provides a test domain-specific language (Selenese) to write tests in a number of popular programming languages, including C#, Java, Groovy, Perl, PHP, Python, and Ruby. The client API runs on the webdriver and the Grid is an additional tool.

- **Ranorex**: Ranorex is a Windows GUI test automation framework for testing many different application types including Web 2.0 applications, Win32, MFC, WPF, Flash/Flex, .NET, and Java (SWT).

- **Test Complete**: Test Complete is an automated testing tool, developed by SmartBear Software which aims to allow testers to create software quality tests. Test Complete is used for testing many different application types including Web, Windows, WPF, Flash, Flex, Silverlight, .NET, and Java.

In all the preceding tools, Selenium and Ranorex are open source. Whereas the rest are paid and commercial tools.

The only one of the preceding tool above which partially supports both UI and Service automation is VSTS but it is too costly and doesn't have a variety of functionality supported when it comes to automation of web services.

So to enable SoapUI and Selenium to work under a single umbrella, we need to integrate them together to achieve Multilayer test automation.

Let's have a look at how to do this in the following section.

SoapUI and Selenium integration

To integrate SoapUI with Selenium and work on creating scripts with it, we need the following prerequisites:

- Java 1.7 (preferably the latest version)
- Selenium Jars 2.0 or webdriver
- Object Inspectors, for example, Firebug or Fire path which are add-ons for Firefox
- Groovy script Jars
- Any browser supported by Selenium and compatible with the version used.

Now let's start with Selenium integration with SoapUI:

1. Download `Selenium.jar` files from the following link, shown in the image:

    `http://www.seleniumhq.org/download/`

2. Download the Java language version of the Jars, once that is done a ZIP folder should be downloaded onto your PC.

3. Unzip the Selenium – Java-'version no' folder.

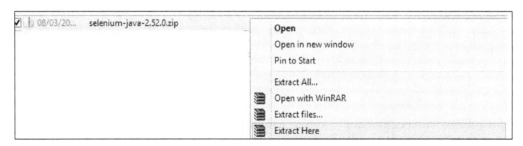

4. Open the unzipped folder.

Name	Type	Compressed size	Password ...	Size
libs	File folder			
CHANGELOG	File	31 KB	No	85 KB
LICENSE	File	4 KB	No	12 KB
NOTICE	File	1 KB	No	1 KB
selenium-java-2.47.1	Executable Jar File	3,678 KB	No	3,774 KB
selenium-java-2.47.1-srcs	Executable Jar File	585 KB	No	663 KB

5. Copy the `selenium-java-2.52.0.jar` and `selenium-java-2.52.0-srcs.jar` from the folder.

6. Open the SoapUI directory folder (In the previous chapter I opted for a default location, such as `C:\Project\SoapUI`. Refer to this location).

7. Place these jars in the following locations: `ext` folder and `lib` folders please refer to the following screenshots for the complete path:

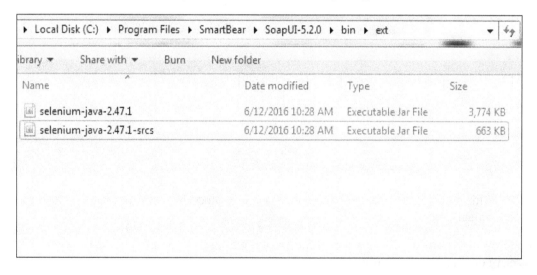

8. Once you have pasted the Jars in the `ext` folder you also need to paste them in the `lib` folder of SoapUI as well.

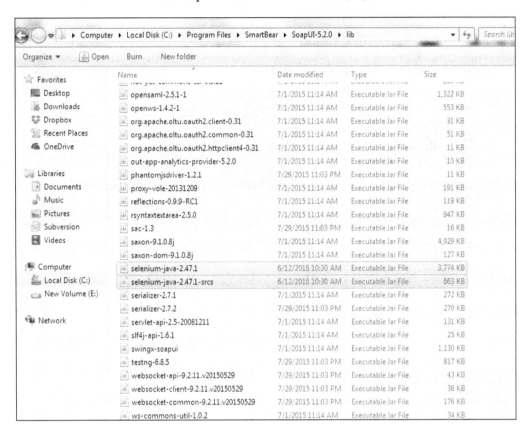

After this step we are done with the setup we now need to work on the Groovy script.

Following is sample Groovy script for invoking a UI from SoapUI using Groovy script enabled by Selenium Jars:

```
import com.eviware.soapui.model.*
import com.eviware.soapui.model.testsuite.Assertable
import com.eviware.soapui.support.XmlHolder
import java.io.File;
def regLogger = org.apache.log4j.Logger.getLogger("RegressionTestLog
er");
```

```
def groovyUtils = new com.eviware.soapui.support.GroovyUtils( context
)
def properties = new java.util.Properties();
import org.openqa.selenium.remote.CapabilityType;
import org.openqa.selenium.remote.DesiredCapabilities;
import com.thoughtworks.selenium.Selenium;

WebDriver driver = new FirefoxDriver();
driver.manage().deleteAllCookies();
driver.manage().window().maximize();
   WebDriver driver = new FirefoxDriver();
   driver.get("http://www.google.com ");
```

The preceding script loads the relevant Jar and then invokes a Firefox driver or the driver of the chosen browser which invokes the URL.

It should also be noted that the version number of Selenium and the browser should be as per the following matrix.

For Windows, the following matrix shows compatibility with Firefox and Selenium versions:

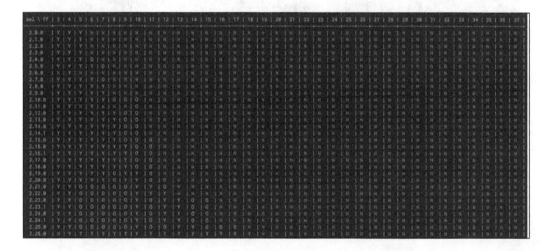

For Linux, see the following compatibility matrix:

```
sso tests/selenium-firefox-support-matrix git:master >>> python collect_results.py Linux
+------+---+---+---+---+---+---+---+----+----+----+----+----+----+----+----+----+----+----+----+----+
| sel \ ff | 3 | 4 | 5 | 6 | 7 | 8 | 9 | 10 | 11 | 12 | 13 | 14 | 15 | 16 | 17 | 18 | 19 | 20 | 21 | 22 |
+------+---+---+---+---+---+---+---+----+----+----+----+----+----+----+----+----+----+----+----+----+
| 2.0.0  | O | O | N | ? | ? | ? | ? | ?  | ?  | ?  | ?  | ?  | ?  | ?  | ?  | ?  | ?  | ?  | ?  | ?  |
| 2.1.0  | O | O | O | ? | ? | ? | ? | ?  | ?  | ?  | ?  | ?  | ?  | ?  | ?  | ?  | ?  | ?  | ?  | ?  |
| 2.2.0  | O | O | O | ? | ? | ? | ? | ?  | ?  | ?  | ?  | ?  | ?  | ?  | ?  | ?  | ?  | ?  | ?  | ?  |
| 2.3.0  | O | O | O | ? | ? | ? | ? | ?  | ?  | ?  | ?  | ?  | ?  | ?  | ?  | ?  | ?  | ?  | ?  | ?  |
| 2.4.0  | N | O | O | O | ? | ? | ? | ?  | ?  | ?  | ?  | ?  | ?  | ?  | ?  | ?  | ?  | ?  | ?  | ?  |
| 2.5.0  | N | O | O | O | O | ? | ? | ?  | ?  | ?  | ?  | ?  | ?  | ?  | ?  | ?  | ?  | ?  | ?  | ?  |
| 2.6.0  | O | O | O | O | O | ? | ? | ?  | ?  | ?  | ?  | ?  | ?  | ?  | ?  | ?  | ?  | ?  | ?  | ?  |
| 2.7.0  | O | O | O | O | O | O | ? | ?  | ?  | ?  | ?  | ?  | ?  | ?  | ?  | ?  | ?  | ?  | ?  | ?  |
| 2.8.0  | O | O | O | O | O | O | ? | ?  | ?  | ?  | ?  | ?  | ?  | ?  | ?  | ?  | ?  | ?  | ?  | ?  |
| 2.9.0  | N | O | O | O | O | O | ? | ?  | ?  | ?  | ?  | ?  | ?  | ?  | ?  | ?  | ?  | ?  | ?  | ?  |
| 2.10.0 | O | O | O | O | O | O | O | O  | O  | ?  | ?  | ?  | ?  | ?  | ?  | ?  | ?  | ?  | ?  | ?  |
| 2.11.0 | N | O | O | O | O | O | O | O  | O  | ?  | ?  | ?  | ?  | ?  | ?  | ?  | ?  | ?  | ?  | ?  |
| 2.12.0 | N | O | O | O | O | O | O | O  | O  | ?  | ?  | ?  | ?  | ?  | ?  | ?  | ?  | ?  | ?  | ?  |
| 2.13.0 | O | O | O | O | O | O | O | O  | O  | ?  | ?  | ?  | ?  | ?  | ?  | ?  | ?  | ?  | ?  | ?  |
| 2.14.0 | O | O | O | O | O | O | O | O  | O  | ?  | ?  | ?  | ?  | ?  | ?  | ?  | ?  | ?  | ?  | ?  |
| 2.14.1 | O | O | O | O | O | O | O | O  | O  | ?  | ?  | ?  | ?  | ?  | ?  | ?  | ?  | ?  | ?  | ?  |
| 2.15.0 | O | O | O | O | O | O | O | O  | O  | O  | ?  | ?  | ?  | ?  | ?  | ?  | ?  | ?  | ?  | ?  |
| 2.16.0 | O | O | O | O | O | O | O | O  | O  | O  | ?  | ?  | ?  | ?  | ?  | ?  | ?  | ?  | ?  | ?  |
| 2.16.1 | N | O | O | O | O | O | O | O  | O  | O  | ?  | ?  | ?  | ?  | ?  | ?  | ?  | ?  | ?  | ?  |
| 2.17.0 | O | O | O | O | O | O | O | O  | O  | O  | ?  | ?  | ?  | ?  | ?  | ?  | ?  | ?  | ?  | ?  |
| 2.18.0 | N | O | O | O | O | O | O | O  | O  | O  | ?  | ?  | ?  | ?  | ?  | ?  | ?  | ?  | ?  | ?  |
| 2.19.0 | ? | O | O | O | O | O | O | O  | O  | O  | N  | N  | N  | N  | N  | N  | N  | N  | N  | N  |
| 2.20.0 | N | O | O | O | O | O | O | O  | O  | O  | O  | ?  | ?  | ?  | ?  | ?  | ?  | ?  | ?  | ?  |
| 2.21.0 | O | O | O | O | O | O | O | O  | O  | O  | O  | O  | ?  | ?  | ?  | ?  | ?  | ?  | ?  | ?  |
| 2.22.0 | N | O | O | O | O | O | O | O  | O  | O  | O  | O  | O  | ?  | ?  | ?  | ?  | ?  | ?  | ?  |
| 2.23.0 | N | O | O | O | O | O | O | O  | O  | O  | O  | O  | O  | ?  | ?  | ?  | ?  | ?  | ?  | ?  |
| 2.23.1 | N | O | O | O | O | O | O | O  | O  | O  | O  | O  | O  | ?  | ?  | ?  | ?  | ?  | ?  | ?  |
| 2.24.0 | N | O | O | O | O | O | O | O  | O  | O  | O  | O  | O  | O  | ?  | ?  | ?  | ?  | ?  | ?  |
| 2.24.1 | N | O | O | O | O | O | O | O  | O  | O  | O  | O  | O  | O  | ?  | ?  | ?  | ?  | ?  | ?  |
| 2.25.0 | N | O | O | O | O | O | O | O  | O  | O  | O  | O  | O  | O  | O  | ?  | ?  | ?  | ?  | ?  |
| 2.26.0 | ? | O | O | O | O | O | O | O  | O  | O  | O  | O  | O  | O  | O  | O  | ?  | ?  | ?  | ?  |
| 2.27.0 | ? | O | O | O | O | O | O | O  | O  | O  | O  | O  | O  | O  | O  | O  | ?  | ?  | ?  | ?  |
| 2.28.0 | ? | O | O | O | O | O | O | O  | O  | O  | O  | O  | O  | O  | O  | O  | ?  | ?  | ?  | ?  |
| 2.29.0 | ? | O | O | O | O | O | O | O  | O  | O  | O  | O  | O  | O  | O  | O  | ?  | ?  | ?  | ?  |
| 2.30.0 | ? | O | O | O | O | O | O | O  | O  | O  | O  | O  | O  | O  | O  | O  | O  | ?  | ?  | ?  |
| 2.31.0 | ? | O | O | O | O | O | O | O  | O  | O  | O  | O  | O  | O  | O  | O  | O  | O  | O  | O  |
| 2.32.0 | ? | O | O | O | O | O | O | O  | O  | O  | O  | O  | O  | O  | O  | O  | O  | O  | O  | O  |
+------+---+---+---+---+---+---+---+----+----+----+----+----+----+----+----+----+----+----+----+----+
```

Also you may look for more details in the changelog at the following URL:

`https://github.com/SeleniumHQ/selenium/blob/master/java/CHANGELOG`

Here is the matrix for Mac:

```
sso tests/selenium-firefox-support-matrix git:master >>> python collect_results.py Mac
+--------+---+---+---+---+---+---+---+----+----+----+----+----+----+----+----+----+----+----+----+----+
| sel \ ff | 3 | 4 | 5 | 6 | 7 | 8 | 9 | 10 | 11 | 12 | 13 | 14 | 15 | 16 | 17 | 18 | 19 | 20 | 21 | 22 |
+--------+---+---+---+---+---+---+---+----+----+----+----+----+----+----+----+----+----+----+----+----+
| 2.0.0  | N | O | N | N | N | N | N | N  | N  | N  | N  | N  | N  | N  | N  | N  | N  | N  | N  | N  |
| 2.1.0  | N | O | O | N | N | N | N | N  | N  | N  | N  | N  | N  | N  | N  | N  | N  | N  | N  | N  |
| 2.2.0  | N | O | N | N | N | N | N | N  | N  | N  | N  | N  | N  | N  | N  | N  | N  | N  | N  | N  |
| 2.3.0  | N | O | O | N | N | N | N | N  | N  | N  | N  | N  | N  | N  | N  | N  | N  | N  | N  | N  |
| 2.4.0  | N | O | N | O | N | N | N | N  | N  | N  | N  | N  | N  | N  | N  | N  | N  | N  | N  | N  |
| 2.5.0  | N | O | O | O | O | N | N | N  | N  | N  | N  | N  | N  | N  | N  | N  | N  | N  | N  | N  |
| 2.6.0  | N | O | O | O | O | N | N | N  | N  | N  | N  | N  | N  | N  | N  | N  | N  | N  | N  | N  |
| 2.7.0  | N | O | O | O | O | N | N | N  | N  | N  | N  | N  | N  | N  | N  | N  | N  | N  | N  | N  |
| 2.8.0  | N | O | N | O | O | N | N | N  | N  | N  | N  | N  | N  | N  | N  | N  | N  | N  | N  | N  |
| 2.9.0  | N | O | N | O | O | N | N | N  | N  | N  | N  | N  | N  | N  | N  | N  | N  | N  | N  | N  |
| 2.10.0 | N | O | O | N | O | O | O | O  | O  | N  | N  | N  | N  | N  | N  | N  | N  | N  | N  | N  |
| 2.11.0 | N | O | O | O | O | O | O | O  | O  | N  | N  | N  | N  | N  | N  | N  | N  | N  | N  | N  |
| 2.12.0 | N | O | O | O | O | O | O | O  | O  | N  | N  | N  | N  | N  | N  | N  | N  | N  | N  | N  |
| 2.13.0 | N | O | O | O | O | O | O | O  | O  | N  | N  | N  | N  | N  | N  | N  | N  | N  | N  | N  |
| 2.14.0 | N | O | O | O | O | O | N | O  | O  | N  | N  | N  | N  | N  | N  | N  | N  | N  | N  | N  |
| 2.14.1 | N | O | O | O | O | O | O | O  | O  | N  | N  | N  | N  | N  | N  | N  | N  | N  | N  | N  |
| 2.15.0 | N | O | O | O | O | O | O | O  | O  | O  | N  | N  | N  | N  | N  | N  | N  | N  | N  | N  |
| 2.16.0 | N | O | O | O | O | O | O | O  | O  | O  | N  | N  | N  | N  | N  | N  | N  | N  | N  | N  |
| 2.16.1 | N | O | O | O | O | O | O | O  | O  | O  | N  | N  | N  | N  | N  | N  | N  | N  | N  | N  |
| 2.17.0 | N | O | O | O | O | O | O | O  | O  | O  | N  | N  | N  | N  | N  | N  | N  | N  | N  | N  |
| 2.18.0 | N | O | O | O | O | O | O | O  | O  | O  | N  | N  | N  | N  | N  | N  | N  | N  | N  | N  |
| 2.19.0 | N | O | O | O | O | O | O | O  | O  | O  | N  | N  | N  | N  | N  | N  | N  | N  | N  | N  |
| 2.20.0 | N | O | O | O | O | O | O | O  | O  | O  | O  | N  | N  | N  | N  | N  | N  | N  | N  | N  |
| 2.21.0 | N | O | O | O | O | O | O | O  | N  | O  | O  | O  | N  | N  | N  | N  | N  | N  | N  | N  |
| 2.22.0 | N | O | O | O | O | O | O | O  | O  | O  | O  | O  | O  | N  | N  | N  | N  | N  | N  | N  |
| 2.23.0 | N | O | O | O | O | O | O | O  | O  | O  | O  | O  | O  | O  | N  | N  | N  | N  | N  | N  |
| 2.23.1 | N | O | O | O | O | O | O | O  | O  | O  | O  | O  | O  | O  | N  | N  | N  | N  | N  | N  |
| 2.24.0 | N | O | O | O | O | O | O | O  | O  | O  | O  | O  | O  | O  | N  | N  | N  | N  | N  | N  |
| 2.24.1 | N | O | O | O | O | O | O | O  | O  | O  | O  | O  | O  | O  | N  | N  | N  | N  | N  | N  |
| 2.25.0 | N | O | O | O | O | O | O | O  | O  | O  | O  | O  | O  | O  | O  | O  | N  | N  | N  | N  |
| 2.26.0 | N | O | O | O | O | O | O | O  | O  | O  | O  | N  | O  | O  | O  | O  | N  | N  | N  | N  |
| 2.27.0 | N | O | O | O | O | O | O | O  | O  | O  | O  | O  | O  | O  | O  | N  | N  | N  | N  | N  |
| 2.28.0 | N | O | O | O | O | O | O | O  | O  | O  | O  | O  | O  | O  | O  | O  | N  | N  | N  | N  |
| 2.29.0 | N | O | O | O | O | O | O | O  | O  | O  | O  | O  | O  | O  | O  | O  | N  | N  | N  | N  |
| 2.30.0 | N | O | O | O | O | O | O | O  | O  | O  | O  | O  | O  | O  | O  | O  | N  | N  | N  | N  |
| 2.31.0 | N | O | O | O | O | O | O | O  | O  | O  | O  | O  | O  | O  | N  | O  | O  | N  | N  | N  |
| 2.32.0 | N | O | O | O | O | O | O | O  | O  | O  | O  | O  | O  | N  | O  | O  | O  | O  | O  | N  |
+--------+---+---+---+---+---+---+---+----+----+----+----+----+----+----+----+----+----+----+----+----+
```

More details on the latest matrix can be seen online at the following link:

https://recordnotfound.com/selenium-firefox-support-matrix-santiycr-120024

Now we have seen how to run our UI test in the Firefox browser, if a need arises to run the test on IE or Chrome, how should we achieve it?

Let's take it step-by-step.

Automation in Google Chrome

For automation in Google Chrome you need to install the chrome driver.

The following screenshot displays the location of the download:

Here is the URL: `http://chromedriver.storage.googleapis.com/index.html?path=2.21/`

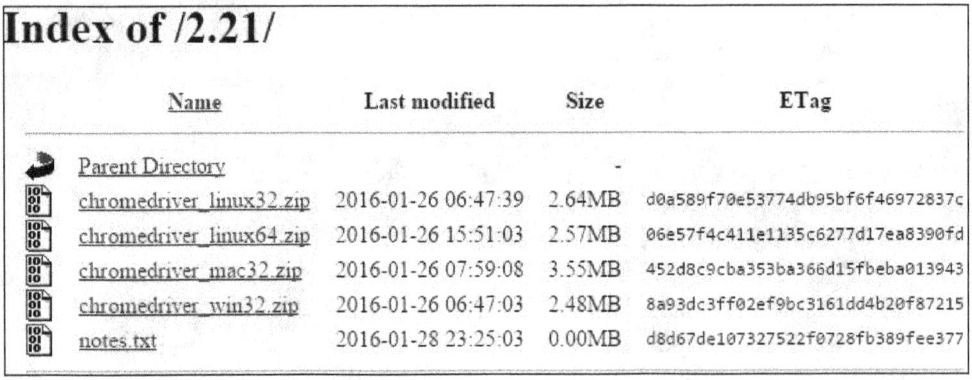

Index of /2.21/

	Name	Last modified	Size	ETag
	Parent Directory		-	
	chromedriver_linux32.zip	2016-01-26 06:47:39	2.64MB	d0a589f70e53774db95bf6f46972837c
	chromedriver_linux64.zip	2016-01-26 15:51:03	2.57MB	06e57f4c411e1135c6277d17ea8390fd
	chromedriver_mac32.zip	2016-01-26 07:59:08	3.55MB	452d8c9cba353ba366d15fbeba013943
	chromedriver_win32.zip	2016-01-26 06:47:03	2.48MB	8a93dc3ff02ef9bc3161dd4b20f87215
	notes.txt	2016-01-28 23:25:03	0.00MB	d8d67de107327522f0728fb389fee377

Once downloaded you need to install the Chrome driver and set the path of the chrome driver in the path of the system.

Once the Chrome driver is up, the following screen will be displayed:

```
Starting ChromeDriver 2.21.371459 (36d3d07f660ff2bc1bf28a75d1cdabed0983e7c4) on
port 9515
Only local connections are allowed.
```

Once the screen is displayed you can now start automating your test using the chrome browser.

Also, before working on the chrome browser make sure you have downloaded the chrome driver which is compatible with your Selenium version and your browser.

You can find compatibility details at the following website:

`https://sites.google.com/a/chromium.org/chromedriver/`

Just for reference, the following is a sample script for UI automation using the Chrome driver:

```
import org.openqa.selenium.*;
import org.openqa.selenium.JavascriptExecutor;
import org.openqa.selenium.firefox.FirefoxDriver;
import org.openqa.selenium.interactions.Actions;
import org.openqa.selenium.ie.InternetExplorerDriver;
import com.eviware.soapui.model.*
import org.openqa.selenium.chrome.ChromeDriver;
import com.eviware.soapui.model.testsuite.Assertable
import com.eviware.soapui.support.XmlHolder
import java.io.File;
//import java.util.*;
//import jxl.write.*
//import jxl.*
def regLogger =
  org.apache.log4j.Logger.getLogger("RegressionTestLoger");
def groovyUtils = new com.eviware.soapui.support.GroovyUtils(
  context )
def properties = new java.util.Properties();
import org.openqa.selenium.remote.CapabilityType;
import org.openqa.selenium.remote.DesiredCapabilities;
import com.thoughtworks.selenium.Selenium;

//System.setProperty("webdriver.chrome.driver", "C:\\Program
  Files\\SmartBear\\SoapUI-5.0.0\\bin\\ext\\chromedriver.exe");
//WebDriver driver = new ChromeDriver();
                    driver.manage().deleteAllCookies();
  driver.get("http://www.google.com ");
```

In the preceding script we use the chrome driver to run the test on the chrome browser.

Working with the IE browser

In case you want your UI to open up in IE, you would need an IE server which can be downloaded from the following location:

```
http://www.seleniumhq.org/download/
```

Once that is done, you need to run the IE server and configure the path of the server in your system.

In case any additional information is to be required on the IE driver, the following link should be referred to:

```
https://github.com/SeleniumHQ/selenium/wiki/
InternetExplorerDriver#required-configuration
```

Following is a sample script for test automation on the IE browser:

```
import org.openqa.selenium.*;
import org.openqa.selenium.JavascriptExecutor;
import org.openqa.selenium.firefox.FirefoxDriver;
import org.openqa.selenium.interactions.Actions;
import org.openqa.selenium.ie.InternetExplorerDriver;
import com.eviware.soapui.model.*
import org.openqa.selenium.chrome.ChromeDriver;
import com.eviware.soapui.model.testsuite.Assertable
import com.eviware.soapui.support.XmlHolder
import java.io.File;
```

```
def regLogger =
  org.apache.log4j.Logger.getLogger("RegressionTestLoger");
def groovyUtils = new com.eviware.soapui.support.GroovyUtils( context
)
def properties = new java.util.Properties();
import org.openqa.selenium.remote.CapabilityType;
import org.openqa.selenium.remote.DesiredCapabilities;
import com.thoughtworks.selenium.Selenium;


File file = new File("C:\\Program Files\\SmartBear\\SoapUI-5.0.0\\
bin\\ext\\IEDriverServer_x64_2.39.0\\IEDriverServer.exe");
System.setProperty("webdriver.ie.driver", file.getAbsolutePath());
WebDriver driver = new InternetExplorerDriver()
```

Implementing a real world test case using SoapUI and Selenium together

Scenario: Verify if a customer is able to pay his credit card bill.

The Flow as follows:

1. User logs in.
2. User enters details on the UI page and clicks **Submit**; a unique ID is generated and shown on the UI with status: in Progress, and asks for a token to process the payment.
3. Service A is called and the request of service A needs the unique ID generated to be passed in the request.
4. Service B is called.
5. Service C creates the new token.
6. The user needs the token created by service C to complete the transaction as he needs to enter it in the UI.
7. The user enters the token and clicks on the **Submit** button.
8. The user receives a message payment is done.

So in the previous example we have eight steps, five of the steps are from the UI and three are from the services side. We also see that there is a need to transfer data from the UI to the service request and vice versa.

Now let's assume we need to assert certain UI elements on the screen as well. Now let's map each of the steps.

We would need Selenium invocation and assertion on the UI level, so how do we do that?

We need to find the locator of the element and then assert it.

We have different ways to find a UI element in Selenium, we can use any of the following or whichever suits us the best:

- Identifier
- Id
- Name
- Link
- DOM
- XPath
- CSS
- UI-element

Once we get to an element we can always use assert to validate the content on the UI screen.

Now we know how to assert but how do we enter data in the fields?

For that we use the sendKeys command. Below is an example which will help us understand this better. We should also note that XPath will remain the same for all browsers.

```
WebElement LoginName =
  driver.findElement(By.xpath("//*[@id='loginname']"));
    LoginName.click();
    LoginName.sendKeys("admin");

WebElement Password =
  driver.findElement(By.xpath("//*[@id='passwd']"));
    Password.click();
    Password.sendKeys("admin");

WebElement Login =
  driver.findElement(By.xpath("//*[@id='loginBtn']"));
    Login.click();
WebElement Cardno = driver.findElement(By.xpath("//*[@id='Credit
card Number']"));
    Cardno.click();
    Cardno.sendKeys("1098987654");
```

This way we can enter data in any field on the UI page. Once we have logged into the application and submitted our card details on the screen, we need to click on the Submit button:

```
WebElement SUBMIT=
  driver.findElement(By.xpath("//*[@id='SBTBtn']"));
    SUBMIT.click();
```

As per our scenario, we will receive a unique number in the UI. Let's name it UID.

Now we need to fetch the UID and pass it to the properties file so that we can re-utilize it in the next step which is a test request.

Here is sample code on how to achieve it:

```
def  UID = driver.findElement(By.xpath("//*[@Name='UniqueID']")).get
text();
testRunner.testCase.setPropertyValue("UID",UID.toString());
```

Now you can use this UID throughout your test case. Once this is done, we can parameterize our test request and run it. This will complete step 3 of our scenario.

1. We need to run a service request; we can do that easily using SoapUI.

2. We again need to run the service but we need to save the response in the properties of SoapUI which can be done with Groovy script or property transfer with the help of XPath as we have learnt in the previous chapters. We will save the property name as Token.

3. Now we will return to the browser and get the property details from the SoapUI properties and enter the details in the token field. See the following sample code:

```
def Token = (testRunner.testCase.getPropertyValue("Token"))
    Token.sendKeys(TOKEN);
```

4. Now the user will need to click on the **Submit** button.

5. Once the **Submit** button is clicked on, we need to validate whether the flow was successful or not. This can be achieved using the assert command.

We need to follow three steps to achieve this:

1. Get the Locator to the text where success or failure appears.

2. Use getText(); at the end of the locator and pass the value in a variable.

3. Use the assert command to validate if the value in the variable matches the expected value or not.

Locator identification

So now we have learnt how to automate the UI and services together, but before we end this chapter let's take a look at a tool which helps us find locators easily:

- **Fire Bug**: An add-on for Firefox which helps create a locator
- **Fire Path**: An add-on for Firefox which helps create a locator

The preceding two add-ons can easily be installed in Firefox.

Once the add-on is installed you will see a bug picture on the right-hand side of the browser.

Click on the bug on the browser and you will be able to see Firebug at the bottom of the screen.

Now when you need to find an element click on the arrow highlighted in the following screenshot and place it on the element you need to identify. In this example its the Google search field:

Once you do that, you can see the XPath visible as shown in the following figure:

This technique doesn't work for complex applications where you need to identify your locators by yourself but can be useful most of the time.

And finally to conclude this chapter we come to the summary.

Summary

So finally let's conclude what we have learnt: Multilayer layer testing, Integration of selenium and SoapUI, Locator Identification for UI, Automating Multilayers together using SoapUI and Selenium.

In the next chapter, we will look into integrating SoapUI with Jenkins and HP QC.

7
SoapUI Integration with Jenkins and HP QC

As the world of testing has advanced over the past few years, we have seen testers who can code and developers who can test with the evolution of the software industry. Testing and development have both played a major role. There is always tension and fighting between the development and testing, but let's try to realize that both teams are fighting for the same objective: The delivery of a quality software product to the client. With time, the release cycles of products and budgets have shrunk. Which has shortened the dev and test cycle and hence has raised a need for new roles and technology which can help deliver the product faster and with good quality. It would not be wrong if we say *Quality Assurance has moved towards Business Assurance*.

Before we move ahead, let's see what we will learn in this chapter. We will discuss:

- DevOps
- Jenkins Integration with SoapUI
- HP QC integration with SoapUI

The preceding factors have given birth to DevOps, so what is DevOps? Let's have a look.

DevOps

DevOps is a bit of development, QA, and operations. The following figure might give a better idea:

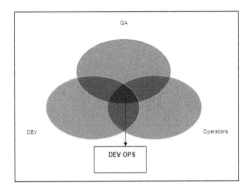

The preceding figure shows that the DevOps team is an intersection of all three major teams.

So as you see in the preceding figure DevOps is a role which is an integration of all three teams in SDLC.

The DevOps Team has good communication with both QA and Dev for the following reasons:

- Development explains to them how the system works and how the deployment scripts should be coded
- QA explains to them how to test the deployed system and write additional tests and automate them
- Operation team keeps them aware of any changes that happen to the system after production

Now let's have a look at how test Automation has a role to play in DevOps.

As we have seen, DevOps people need to write tests with QA that help to validate the build. So here comes the need for test automation. DevOps automate the sanity or smoke test suite and hook it up with any Continuous Integration tools like Jenkins. What happens now is, whenever a new build is built and deployed on any server, the sanity test automatically gets executed and publishes the report to the destined stakeholders.

So here comes the question: how do we integrate SoapUI with Jenkins or bamboo? We have already seen in previous chapters how to create a build.xml file to run SoapUI tests with Ant and generate a report.

We will now see multiple ways to integrate SoapUI test cases with Jenkins

But before moving on to that, lets have a look at what Jenkins is and what it does.

Jenkins

Jenkins is a continuous integration server which creates the build and deploys on the environment. It can also be used as a scheduler where you can schedule your test and build process in a nightly fashion.

Jenkins can also help you achieve code quality by integrating with tools like selenium and SoapUI. Based on the results of the test runs, action could be taken to improve the current build.

Installing Jenkins on Windows

As we know what Jenkins is, let's see how it can be integrated with testing tools. But before that let's see how to setup Jenkins.

Setting up Jenkins on your local machine:

1. Download the `.war` file from: `https://updates.jenkins-ci.org/download/war/`

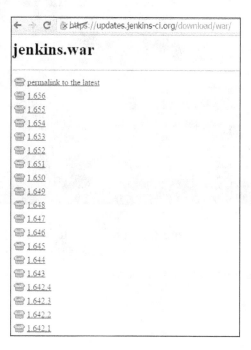

2. Once the .war files are downloaded, open a command prompt and enter the following command:

    ```
    Java -jar  "Path of WAR file"
    ```

3. After typing the command press *Enter*.

4. Verify that the execution begins on the command line:

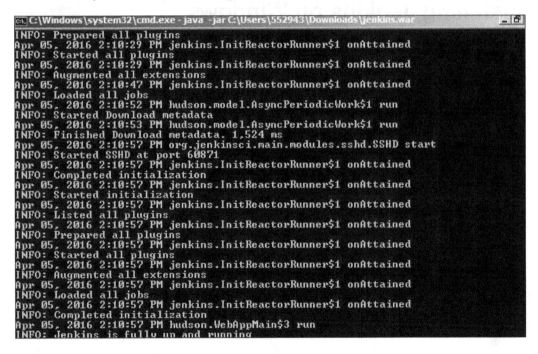

5. Once the execution has begun, it's now time to invoke Jenkins by opening the browser and entering the URL http://localhost:8080/.

6. Verify that the following screen pops up:

The preceding screen proves that we have successfully installed Jenkins on a Windows machine.

Integrating Jenkins with SoapUI

Now as we have installed Jenkins on the machine let's see how we integrate SoapUI with it:

1. Click on **New Item** and select a free style project as shown in the following screenshot:

2. After selecting the project type, click **OK**:

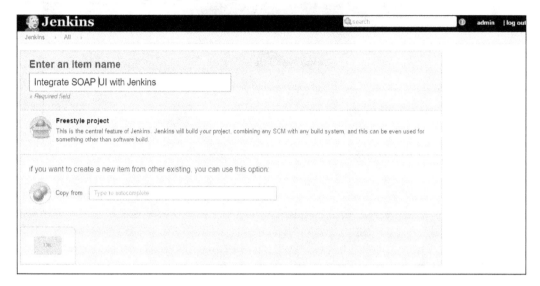

3. After which you will be navigated to the following screen:

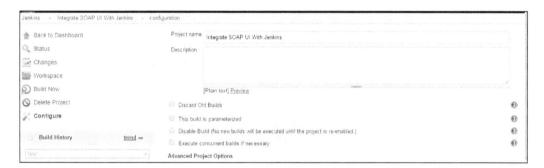

In the preceding screen you can add the description of the project.

4. Configure the source code repositories by using the **Advanced Project** options:

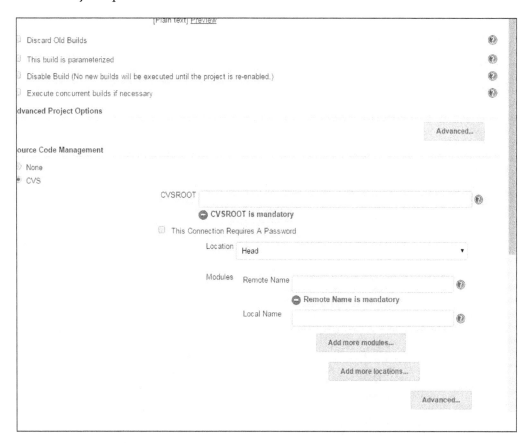

After we have added the source code repository details, your repository is in sync with your tool.

You also have certain other build options which can be useful in configuring your build:

After you have configured your build options, you have now learnt how to integrate your codebase with Jenkins. Now is the time for integrating the test tools.

Integrating the test tools

If you see in the following screenshot, we have several options to add a build step:

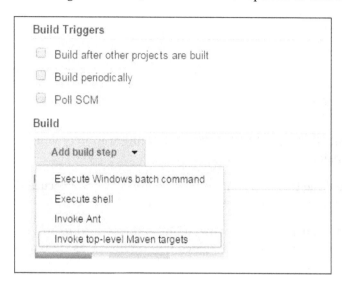

Using Ant: We have in previous chapters seen how can we create a `build.xml` file to execute and generate reports for our Test automation suites. We can use the same `build.xml` file and the same shall work for us.

```
<arg line= "-j -f  'c:\project\SoapUITest ' ' like
   c:/project/SoapUITest  like c:/project/SoapUITest
   /Production.xml'"/>
</exec>
</target>
<target name = "testreport" depends ="soapui">
   <junitreport todir=
     "C:/Users/pnandan/Desktop/Analysis/NewFolder">
     <fileset dir="C:/Users/pnandan/Desktop/Analysis/NewFolder">
       <include name="TEST-TestSuite_1.xml"/>
     </fileset>
     <report todir="C:/Users/Admin / Analysis/Reports /HTML"
         styledir="C:/Testing/apache-ant-1.9.6/etc"
         format="frames">
     </report>
   </junitreport>
</target>
</project>
```

The second option we have is to invoke a batch file. We can use the command line functionality of SoapUI to create a batch file which executes the project:

```
Commandline utility of soap UI
Sample Batch file:


cd C:\Program Files\SmartBear\soapUI-4.0.1\bin testrunner.bat
-ehttps://192.90.190.19:7001/test?wsdl -sTestSuite -r -a -fC:\Users\
pnandan\Desktop\batchsoap -I "C:\Users\pnandan\Desktop\batsoap\
soapuitestproject.xml"
```

Use the batch file and enter the details of the configuration of your project and name it with an extension `.bat`.

Once you have done that you can pass the reference in the **Execute Windows batch command** option displayed in the preceding screenshot.

Now to integrate it using the same batch file, you just need to add the batch file content to the execute Windows batch file command, as shown in the following screenshot.

The following screenshot shows how you can add the batch file and run SoapUI from Jenkins:

Let's also have a look at the command line options available:

- a: Returns all test results, not only errors
- A: Returns results using folders instead of long names
- c: This can be used to select the specified test cases to be run

- D: Sets system property with `name=value`
- d: The domain to use in any authentications, overrides any domain set for any `TestRequests`
- e: Sets the endpoint to be used
- f: Specifies the root folder to which test results should be exported
- G: Sets global property with name=value
- h: The `host:port` to use when invoking `test-requests`, overrides only the host part of the endpoint set in the project file
- I: Do not stop if error occurs, ignore them
- i: Enables SoapUI UI-related components
- j: Turns on exporting of JUnit-compatible reports
- M: Creates a Test Run Report in XML format
- m: Sets the threshold value for test step errors
- P: Sets project property with name value pair
- p: The password to use in any authentication
- r: Turns on printing of a small summary report
- S: Sets to save the project file after tests have been run
- s: Used to select the test suite to run
- t: Sets the `soapui-settings.xml` file
- u: The username to use in any authentication
- v: Sets password for `soapui-settings.xml` file
- w: Sets the WSS password type
- x: Sets project password

So now we have seen two possible ways to integrate SoapUI or any other tool with Jenkins using Ant and a batch file.

Once we are done with integrating the tool now is the time to see what can be done post-test case execution.

Post execution steps

Once you have done the execution step you may want to decide to perform additional steps. For that you have options in **Add post-build action**.

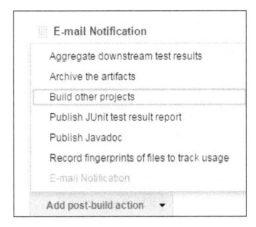

Let's have a look at some of the options that can be useful to us:

- **Build other projects**: This option can be used to run another ant task which could be to revert the build in case most of the test cases have failed
- **Publish JUnit style report**: This option is used to build a JUnit style report
- **E-mail Notification**: Publish an e-mail to the stakeholders with the results of the test run with build deployed or reverted status

This gives us a view of end to end use of Jenkins with respect to integration with SoapUI.

Integrating with test management tools

With the Test Automation phase of Software Testing Life Cycle showing tremendous increase in the ROI, project leaders want to get more and more out of it, which has laid the foundations of more areas which can be covered as part of test automation.

Tracking the results of the Test automation runs has always been a tedious job, it is very important to keep track of such metrics since they can be used to track the build cycle automation suite performance, defect metrics, and so on.

So to avoid manual effort of updating the test results in Test management tools, testers have come up with innovative solutions to automate the process of updating the test management tools with the test automation results status.

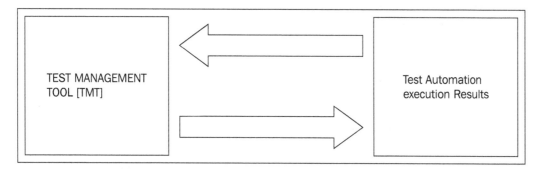

Updating of Test results can be triggered from the Automation suite as well as from the Test management tool as shown in the figure preceding.

So, in the Test Management Tool, when you run any test case it runs the Test Automation suite and updates QC automatically. Or, if you run the Test Automation suite it updates the test case status in QC automatically.

So let's see how we do that.

Let take a look at the top two test management tools on the market:

- JIRA with Zephyr: For JIRA integration we have a JIRA Plugin available which only works with the Pro edition of SoapUI which is Ready API

- HP QC: SoapUI open source can still be integrated with QC

 For JIRA plugins visit `https://github.com/SmartBear/ready-jira-plugin`

QC Integration with SoapUI

Dragonfly is the answer to the question; *how do we integrate QC with SoapUI?* so let's see how we update QC with Automation test cases results automatically and vice versa.

1. Download Dragonfly from the following link:

   `http://www.agiletestware.com/dragonfly`

While installing Dragonfly, please provide the directory to be installed as the `bin` directory of SoapUI.

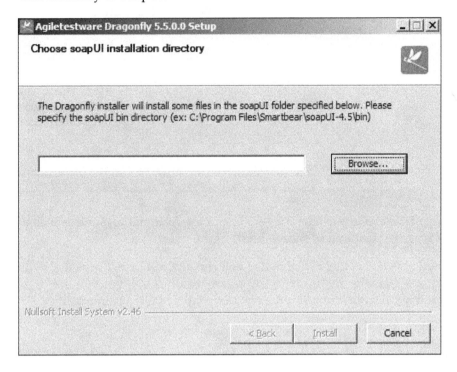

2. Now you need to create the following custom properties at project level in SoapUI:

   ° QC_URL
   ° QC_Domain
   ° QC_Project
   ° QC_User
   ° QC_Password
   ° QC_TestPlanDirectory
   ° QC_TestLabDirectory
   ° QC_soapUI_ARGS
   ° QC_Bulk Update
   ° QC_Run Name
   ° QC_ProjectPath
   ° QC_Export_Disabled_Tests
   ° QC_Dragonfly_Plugin

3. In case you want to create test cases from QC to SoapUI or you want to create tests from SoapUI to QC you can use the following two options

   Before that, create a project in SoapUI and right click on the project level in SoapUI and you can verify that the options for the Dragonfly plugins are now available.

   ° **Dragonfly: Export to HP ALM**: This feature is to create test cases in QC which already reside in SoapUI

   ° **Dragonfly: Import to HP ALM**: This feature allows you to import tests from QC and create tests in SoapUI

   Now if you select any of the features, for example Export to HP ALM you will see the following screen:

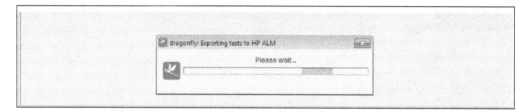

   Which will make sure that the test is now created in HP QC.

4. Now once you have exported your test, you can now run your test normally and on completion the test case results will be updated in HP QC:

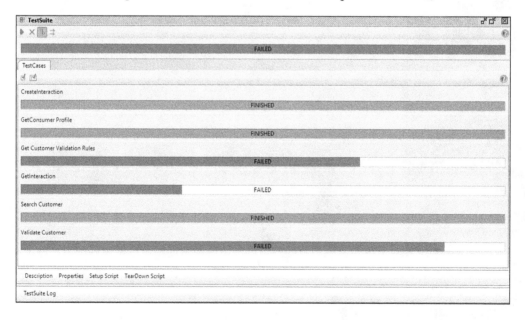

With this we have come to the end of this chapter. Let's see the summary section to see what have we covered in this chapter.

Summary

In this chapter we have discussed DevOps and the way we can achieve it by integrating SoapUI with Jenkins. We have also learnt to integrate SoapUI with Test Management tools like QC.

The next chapter explains how to bring all the tools and plugins learnt in the previous chapters into action, and hook all of them up to SoapUI in a single go.

8
End-to-End Test Automation

In the previous chapter we learned about and studied different automation subjects. Now let's have a look at what we have studied to date:

- Test automation framework creation
- Integration with Jenkins
- Integration with Ant
- Creating reports
- Data-driven frameworks
- Selenium integration
- Different types of frameworks
- Utilities in a test automation framework

- Integration with HP QC

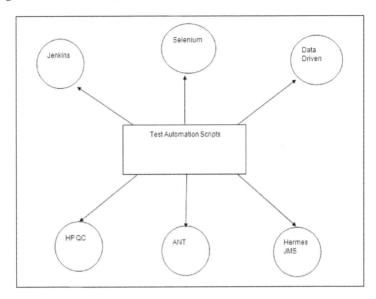

Now let's take a case where we need to integrate all of these together.

Integrating everything together

Requirements of a test automation framework:

- Implementation of continuous integration testing where tests are run each time a build changes or as a business needs.
- An external data source is required to keep test data.
- Integration with test management tools
- The test case has JMS services exposed over IBM MQ so we need a handler for the JMS message. We need reports to be generated and sent by e-mail to destined stakeholders

So, after analyzing the preceding requirements, lets simplify them:

- We need a data-driven framework
- We need to have a solution where we can invoke the UI
- We have an exposed web service so we would need a handler or a tool integration for the same

- We need the test case repository to be updated automatically when automated test runs.

- We need to generate reports and e-mail automatically.

- We need to integrate the framework with tools like Jenkins.

So the big question is how do we do it? Let's take it step-by-step:

1. Data driven framework.

   Solution: we have studied in previous chapters how to data drive a test. Let's revise the way we do it. We need two things:

   ° Groovy script
   ° Excel spreadsheet

   When you create a test case, add a Groovy step, and make this step the very first step in the test case. Second, we need to call the created parameters in the request.

   We can use the following script:

   Excel integration via Groovy script

```
import com.eviware.soapui.model.*
import com.eviware.soapui.model.testsuite.Assertable
import com.eviware.soapui.support.XmlHolder
import java.io.File;
import java.util.*;
import jxl.write.*
import jxl.*
def regLogger =
  org.apache.log4j.Logger.getLogger("RegressionTestLoger");
def groovyUtils = new
  com.eviware.soapui.support.GroovyUtils( context )
def properties = new java.util.Properties();
def s2
def s3=(testRunner.testCase.getPropertyValue("RUN"))
regLogger.info(s3);
if (s3 !=1 & s2 != 1&s3 !=3);
{ testRunner.testCase.setPropertyValue("RUN");
  s3=(testRunner.testCase.getPropertyValue("RUN"));
}
Workbook workbook = Workbook.getWorkbook(new
  File(D:\\testdata.xls)
```

```
for (count in 2..&lt; 11)
{

    Sheet sheet = workbook.getSheet(1)
    Cell a1 = sheet.getCell(0,count) // getCell(row,column) —
    place some values in myfile.xlsCell b2 =
    sheet.getCell(s3.toInteger(),count) // then those values
    will be acessed using a1, b2 &amp; c3 Cell.
    String s1 = a1.getContents();
    s2 = b2.getContents();
    //Cell c2 = sheet.getCell(2,1)
    testRunner.testCase.setPropertyValue(s1,s2);
}
workbook.close()
```

The preceding script will ensure that step 1 (making a data driven framework) is completed. Now let's move to step 2.

2. We need to have an integration with the UI automation tool.

    For this requirement we studied the integration of Selenium with SoapUI in *Chapter 6, Multilayer Test Automation Using SoapUI and Selenium* of this book.

    Create a step, as per the business requirement of the test case, and arrange a step in the sequence in which the case demands.

    The following is a sample script for Selenium integration:

```
import org.openqa.selenium.By
import org.openqa.selenium.WebDriver
import org.openqa.selenium.WebElement
import org.openqa.selenium.firefox.FirefoxDriver
import org.openqa.selenium.support.ui.ExpectedCondition
import org.openqa.selenium.support.ui.WebDriverWait

    WebDriver driver = new FirefoxDriver()

    // And now use this to visit facebook
    driver.get("http://www.Facebook.com")        // Find the
    text input element by its name
    WebElement element =
    driver.findElement(By.name("Login"));   // Enter something
    to search for
```

```
element.sendKeys("pranai!")
```

```
//Close the browser
driver.quit()
```

The preceding scripts will make sure that step 2 is achieved. Now let's move on to step 3.

3. We have a web service, so we would need a handler or a tool integration for the same.

    To achieve step 3, and to send message over JMS in SoapUI, we have Hermes JMS, which can be invoked by clicking on **Tools**.

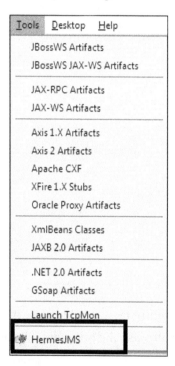

You can use Hermes JMS to connect to any **ESB** (short for **Enterprise Service Bus**). See the following screenshot:

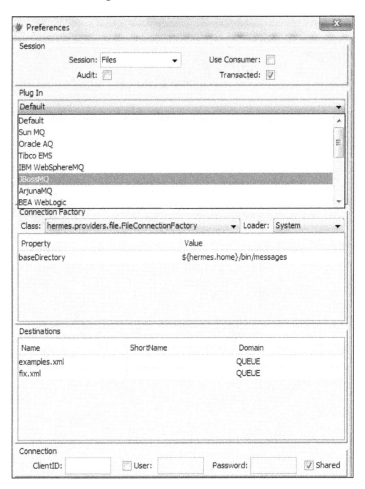

Details of how to configure Hermes JMS are explained in previous chapters.

Alternatively we can also use the following Groovy script to connect to queues and topics:

```
import  com.eviware.soapui.impl.wsdl.submit.transports.jms.
JMSConnectionHolder
import com.eviware.soapui.impl.wsdl.submit.transports.jms.util.
HermesUtils
import com.eviware.soapui.impl.wsdl.submit.transports.jms.
JMSEndpoint
```

```
import hermes.Hermes
import javax.jms.*

def jmsEndpoint = new  JMSEndpoint("jms://activeMQSession::queue::
queueQ1");
def hermes = HermesUtils.getHermes( context.testCase.testSuite.
project, jmsEndpoint.sessionName)
def jmsConnectionHolder = new JMSConnectionHolder( jmsEndpoint,
hermes, false, null ,null ,null);

Session queueSession = jmsConnectionHolder.getSession();
Queue queueSend = jmsConnectionHolder.getQueue(
jmsConnectionHolder.getJmsEndpoint().getSend() );
Queue queueBrowse = jmsConnectionHolder.getQueue(
jmsConnectionHolder.getJmsEndpoint().getReceive() );

MessageProducer messageProducer =queueSession.createProducer(
queueSend );
TextMessage textMessageSend = queueSession.createTextMessage();
textMessageSend.setText( "jms message from groovy");
messageProducer.send( textMessageSend );
textMessageSend.setText( "another jms message from groovy");
messageProducer.send( textMessageSend );

QueueBrowser qb  = queueSession.createBrowser(queueBrowse);
Enumeration en= qb.getEnumeration();
while(en.hasMoreElements()){
    TextMessage tm = (TextMessage)en.nextElement();
    log.info tm.getText()
    }
jmsConnectionHolder.closeAll()
```

4. We need the test case repository to be updated automatically when we have automated test runs.

    Let's assume that we have HP QC as a test management tool. We can use Dragonfly to integrate with SoapUI.

    Details of how to integrate SoapUI with Dragonfly can be found in the previous chapter.

    Let's move to step 5 now.

5. We need to generate reports and e-mail them automatically.

To generate reports and e-mail them we need to use Ant scripts, so we will need to set up Ant and also place a `javamail.jar` file in the `lib` folder of Ant.

The following scripts that can be used to generate reports and send e-mail:

Here is the `build.xml` for generating reports.

```
arg line= "-j -f 'C:/Users/pnandan/Desktop/Analysis/NewFolder'
'C:/Users/pnandan/Desktop/Test/Pranai/Production.xml'"/>
 </exec>
 </target>
 <target name = "testreport" depends ="soapui">
 <junitreport todir="C:/Users/pnandan/Desktop/Analysis/NewFolder">
 <fileset dir="C:/Users/pnandan/Desktop/Analysis/NewFolder">
 <include name="TEST-TestSuite_1.xml"/>
 </fileset>
 <report todir="C:/Users/pnandan/Desktop/Analysis/NewFolder/HTML"
   styledir="C:/Testing/apache-ant-1.9.6/etc"
   format="frames">
 </report>
    </junitreport>
    </target>
   </project>
```

here is the `build.xml` file for sending e-mails:

```
<property name="line2" value="Message"/>
<echo message="${line2}"/>

<mail mailhost="pranainandan08@gmail.com" mailport="25"
subject="Test build" charset="utf-8">
  <from address=" pranainandan08@gmail.com "/>
  <to address="all@xyz.com"/>
  <message>Test Message</message>
</mail>
```

Let's now start integrating with Jenkins:

6. Click on **New Item** and select a free style project as shown in the
   following screen:

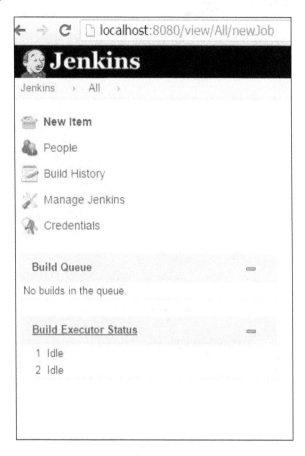

7. After selecting the project type, click on **OK**:

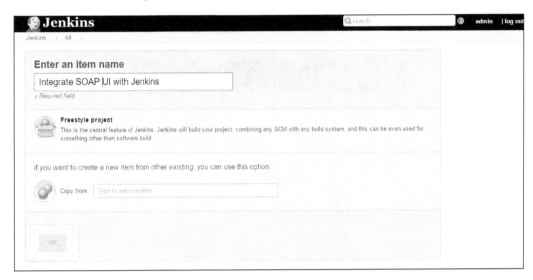

8. After this you will be navigated to the following screen:

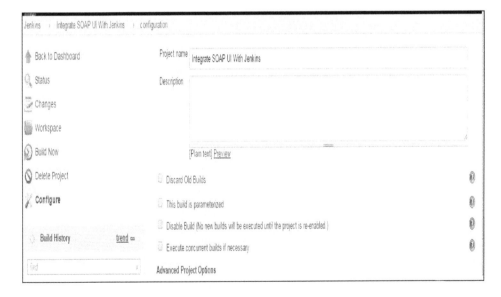

9. Configure the source code repositories by using the **Advanced Project Options**.

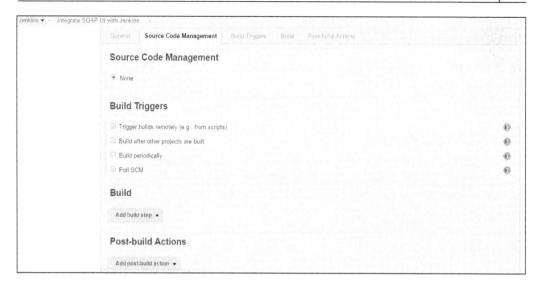

After we have added the source code repository details your repository is in sync with your tool.

You also have certain other **Build** options that can be useful in configuring your build:

For more detailed steps please refer to *Chapter 7, SoapUI Integration with Jenkins and HP QC*.

With this, we have seen that all the steps are addressed with the test automation framework.

Summary

In this chapter we have learned to create end-to-end test automation frameworks by integrating different tools and utilities together. This chapter provides the audience a real-time view of end-to-end automation.

Service Mocking

9

As we move forward with test automation of SOA based applications we face several challenges to automate business flows. A few of these challenges can be answered by service virtualization and service mocking.

Service virtualization is a matured and a more detailed process to help in testing and test automation, whereas in service mocking stubs are made by considering test cases or test suites.

In this chapter we will learn how to create a mock service with different techniques/ dispatch methods and deploy them.

So, before we move forward, we may well ask why we need service virtualization or service mocking.

Let's take a look at a few of the challenges faced during SOA testing and test automation:

- No access to the third-party service
- All the services are not ready, hence integration cannot be tested
- Dependency on an external system which is not in control of the test team
- Cost to be paid for accessing certain systems in the test environment

Because of the preceding issues, most of the time the test cases are not completely executed. To address the challenges we use service mocking or service virtualization techniques.

Now let's see what SoapUI has to offer in this area.

SoapUI offers a service mocking facility in its open source version.

Let's have a look at the advantages of mocking:

- Test sets can be created early
- Early identification of bugs as you get the feel of a live environment via stub
- Testing independent services is possible
- Helps at the time of PoC when we don't have the real environment
- Parallel teams can work at the same time as the developer works on their uncompleted work and QA, mock the uncompleted service and move ahead

So let's see how we create a mock service in SoapUI.

Creating mock services in SoapUI

Lets now see how to create mock services in SoapUI.

A pre-requisite is that the WSDL is already loaded in the project. In the following example, we have loaded the WSDL in the tool:

1. Right click on the binding and verify that below options pop up:

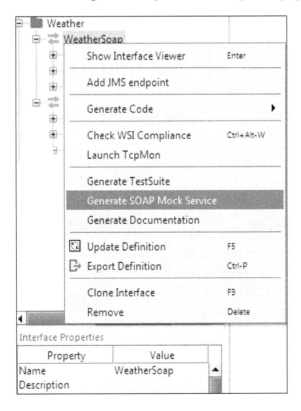

As shown in the figure preceding, select **Generate SOAP Mock Service**.

2. Verify that the options screen below pops up after the user has selected **Generate Mock Service**:

On the preceding screen you can see the option to select a single as well as multiple operations. To mock you can add and configure your service accordingly here such as if you want to configure the path or the port. Click on **OK** to proceed forward.

3. On clicking on **OK** you will be directed to the following page:

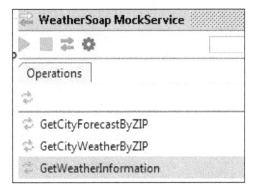

Now on this screen you may select any operation for which you want to further configure your mock stubs. Also from here you can change the configuration of the mock service endpoint and port details by clicking on the ⚙ settings icon and you will see the following configuration window appear:

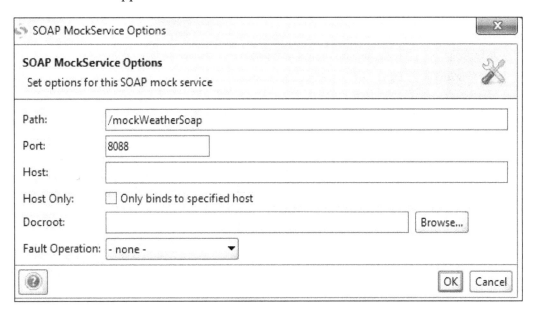

Now let's select the first operation from the previous screen **GetCityForecastByZip**.

4. Once you have clicked on the operation you will be navigated to the following screen:

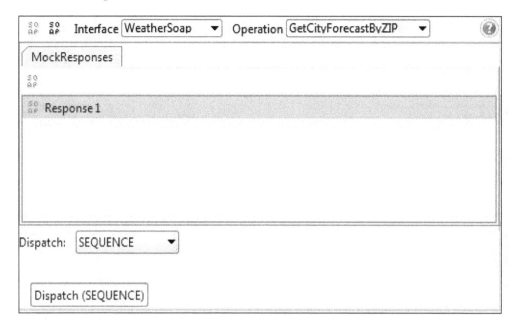

5. On the preceding screen we have a **Dispatch**: option. In the **Dispatch** option dropdown you may select any of the dispatch types based on your stub requirement:

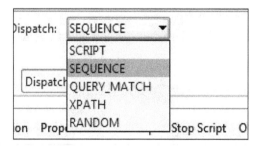

 We will study each dispatch type later in the chapter.

So now if we need to change our response values, or response, how do we change it?

6. Changing the response values: In order to change the response values you need to click on **Response 1** as shown in the following screenshot:

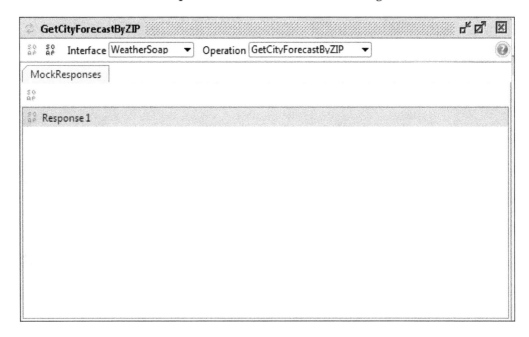

7. Once you click on **Response 1** you will be navigated to the following screen:

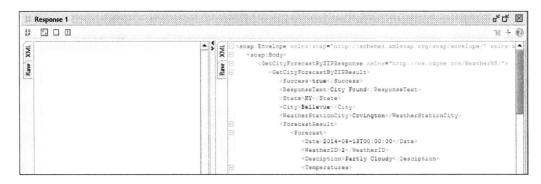

On the preceding screen if you want to change the response you can edit the response data and put any value there, shown in the following screenshot:

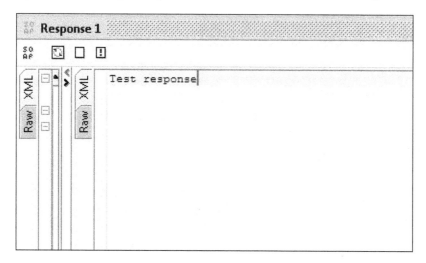

8. Once you have set the response, as per your need, your stub is configured. Now let see how to run the stub:

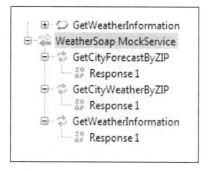

9. Double click on the binding value named **WeatherSoap MockService** and verify that the screen following pops up:

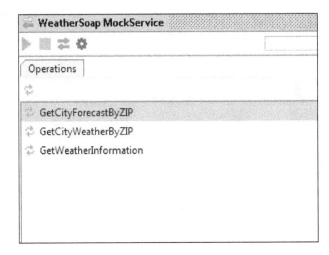

10. On this screen click on the green play button to run the mock service.

11. Now to verify your stub, go to the request editor, open the request and run the request against the correct endpoint:

> **Note:** PUISN001SI-L1 in the following screenshot can be a localhost or the IP of the machine where you want to host the service.

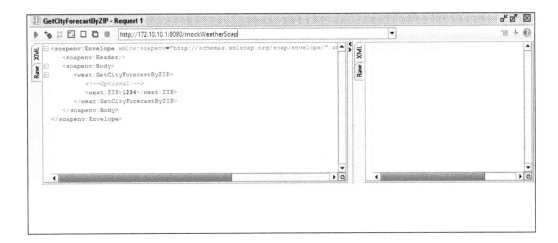

12. Once you run the request you will see the following response:

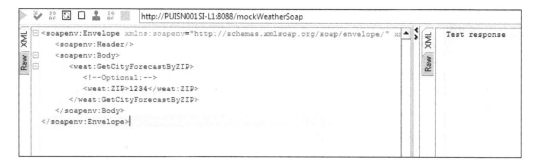

13. Now in order to check if your stub is really working, shut down the stub by clicking on the red button on the following screen:

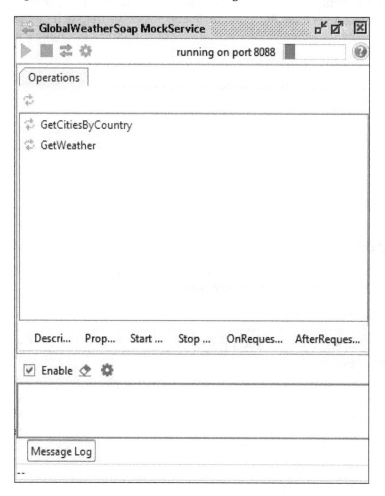

14. Once you have stopped the service, in order to verify if the stub works correctly or not, rerun the service and you will get the following message:

<html><body><p>There are currently 0 running Mock Services</p><ul></ul></p></body></html>

The preceding steps confirm the successful creation of a stub for a particular operation. You can replicate the same steps for creating stubs for other operations as well.

Now let's have a look at a different dispatch method.

Dispatch methods

Dispatch methods provides us with more functionality, flexibility and support to create robust mock services. We can create and select the dispatch method based on our requirements, whether they are simple or complex. Let's have a look at the dispatch method available in the SoapUI mocking feature.

Following are the various dispatch methods:

- Sequence
- Random
- XQuery Match
- XPath
- Script

Sequence

The sequence dispatch method is the most basic of all the five and the responses are returned in the sequence in which they were added.

Let's have look at an example:

On the following screen when you right click, you will receive an option to create a **New MockResponse**.

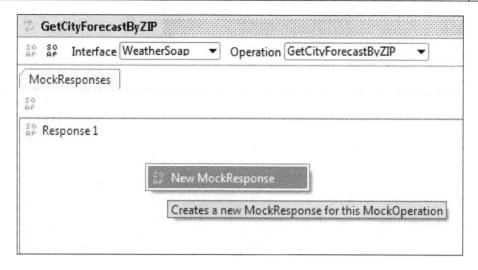

On the previous screen, when you select **New MockResponse,** you may add a new response.

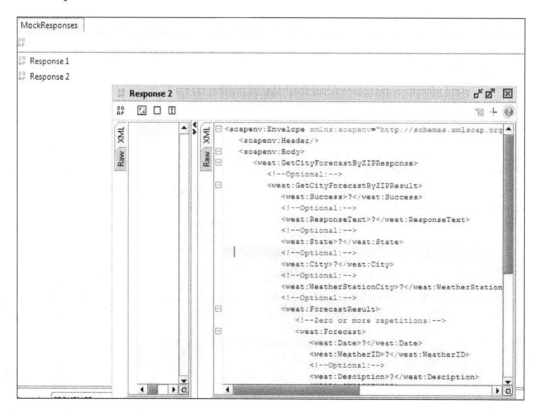

So, as you can see, now you have created two responses for the service.

Both the responses will be called in sequence each time the service is invoked.

Random

the random dispatch method is used to call any response at a given point of time.

If you really don't care which response is returned out of the many created you may use this dispatch type.

The configuration for a random dispatch method is shown following:

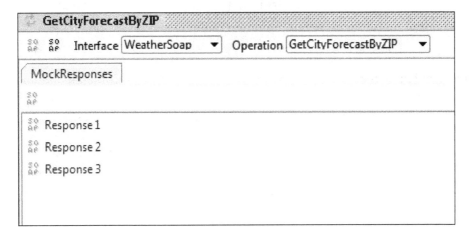

XQuery Match

This is the most powerful dispatch method available. This method provides intelligence to the mock services feature of SoapUI. Using this feature you can create conditional mock services where the response gets populated based on the input received in the request.

Now let's have detailed look at the same.

So to create a mock with XQuery Match, select the option XQuery Match from the dispatch methods dropdown:

Verify that after the selection of the dispatch method you will receive the configuration window for XQuery Match:

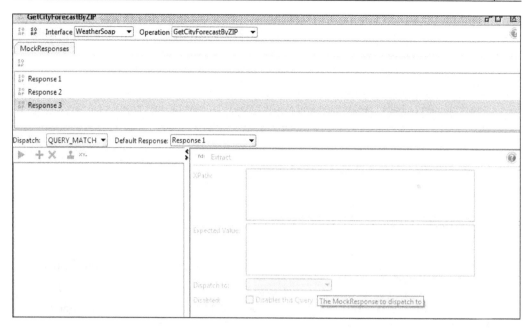

Now the first step should be to create a new match by clicking on the ✛ button and create a match name Zip 1. Repeat this step for the creation of Zip 2 and Zip 3.

Once you have created all of those options you may now choose Zip 1 and move to the configuration window:

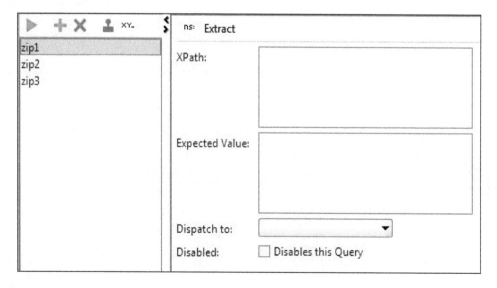

On the previous screen you need to set the XPath of the parameter whose value you want to match, and then, based on the comparison, you may return the response by selecting it from the dispatch to dropdown.

XPath Match: To create an XPath let's have a look at the request XML:

```
<soapenv:Envelope xmlns:soapenv="http://schemas.xmlsoap.org/soap/
envelope/" xmlns:weat="http://ws.cdyne.com/WeatherWS/">
   <soapenv:Header/>
   <soapenv:Body>
      <weat:GetCityForecastByZIP>
         <!--Optional:-->
         <weat:ZIP>1234</weat:ZIP>
      </weat:GetCityForecastByZIP>
   </soapenv:Body>
</soapenv:Envelope>
```

So if we want to create our conditions based on the ZIP parameter values we need the the XPath for ZIP should be:

```
declare namespace soapenv='http://schemas.xmlsoap.org/soap/envelope/';
declare namespace weat='http://ws.cdyne.com/WeatherWS/';
//weat:ZIP/text()
```

So now our expected value should be `1234` ,and out of the three responses we should select **Response 1**:

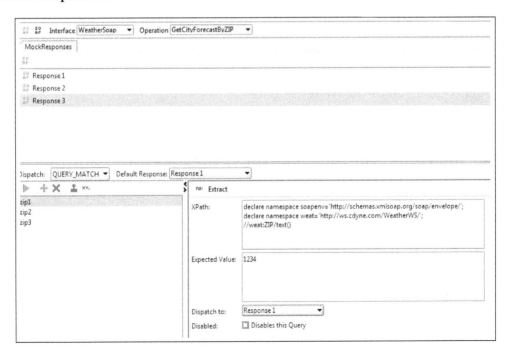

Now replicate the same steps for the Zip 2 and Zip 3 match as well with different expected values.

The expected value of Zip 2 should be 2345 and Zip 3 should be 3456.

Now run the service and you will get the following results for different input data:

Test the request with the input as 1234:

Test request with input as 2345 you will receive the following response:

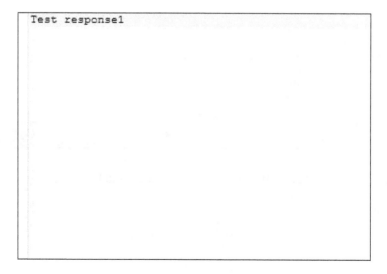

Test the request with the input as 3456:

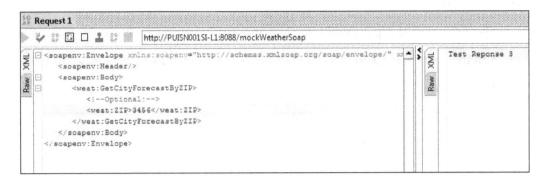

The preceding screenshot verifies the successful creation of a mock service with the XQuery Match dispatch method.

XPath Match

XPath Match is not that powerful compared to XQuery Match, but is similar in nature. It's also used for conditional response selection.

Let's have a look at the configuration of XPath Match:

```
ispatch: XPATH        ▼   Default Response: Response 1        ▼

 1 declare namespace soapenv='http://schemas.xmlsoap.org/soap/envelope/';
 2 declare namespace weat='http://ws.cdyne.com/WeatherWS/';
 3
 4 if (//weat:ZIP[. = '1234']   then
 5     'Response1'
 6     else
 7     if (//weat:ZIP[. = '2345'] then
 8     'Response2'
 9     else
10     'Response3'
```

The preceding screen shows an example of an XPath Match.

Script

Using a Groovy script editor makes the mock service feature very powerful and flexible to use. You may use the Groovy script to create conditional selection and creation *n* number of conditions for your response selection. You may also use an external source for storing the response.

Let's have a look at a sample script for this dispatch method type:

```
import com.eviware.soapui.support.GroovyUtils
import groovy.xml.XmlUtil
log.info 'Script for Dynamic Response Creatuon'
def groovyUtils = new GroovyUtils(context)
def xmlParser = new XmlParser()
def responseContent
def requestXmlHolder =
  groovyUtils.getXmlHolder(mockRequest.getRequestContent())
requestXmlHolder.declareNamespace("Weather","
  http://ws.cdyne.com/WeatherWS/")
requestXmlHolder.declareNamespace("SOAPENV"," http:
  //weat:ZIP/text()")


def ZIP =
  requestXmlHolder.getNodeValue(
  "//test:Quote/QuoteRequest[1]/quoteNumber[1]")
if(quoteNumber == '1234')
{
  responseContent = xmlParser.parse(groovyUtils.projectPath
 +"/responses/Response1.xml")

}
else
{
  responseContent = xmlParser.parse(groovyUtils.projectPath
  +"/responses/Response2.xml")
}
context.content = XmlUtil.serialize(responseContent)
log.info 'complete'
```

Make sure that you set ${content} in the response of the mock service since this will make sure that the value of the response is dynamically generated by the Groovy script.

Also put the so path so that it's picked up from there you can find the project path from the project properties.

The preceding script picks the response from a specified location on the machine, based on the conditions in the script.

Deploying mock services to an external server

We can deploy mock services to any servlet container example: **Tomcat**

To do that we need to extract the WAR file from the SoapUI project and then move the WAR file to Tomcat where it can be accessible to any consumer of the mock service.

Extracting the WAR file:

1. Right click on the project level and verify that following screen is populated:

Show Project View	Enter
Add WSDL	Ctrl-U
Add WADL	Ctrl-F
New REST Service from URI	
Launch TestRunner	
Launch LoadTestRunner	
Launch HTTP Monitor	
Launch Security TestRunner	
New TestSuite	Ctrl-T
New SOAP MockService	Ctrl-O
New REST MockService	Ctrl-R
Rename	F2
Remove	Delete
Reload Project	F5
Resolve	
Close Project	
Save Project	Ctrl-S
Save Project As	Ctrl+Shift-S
Export Project	
Import Test Suite	
Import Mock Service	
Deploy As War	
Start HermesJMS	

2. On the preceding screen select the option **Deploy As War**.

3. Verify that the user is presented with the following popup:

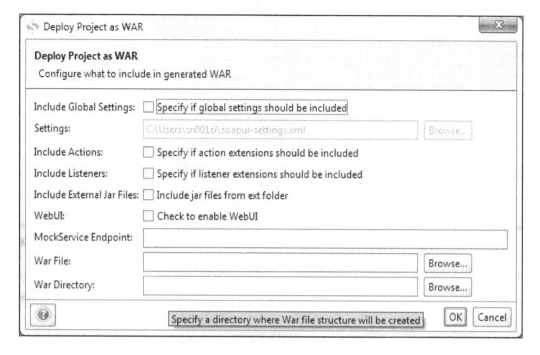

4. On the preceding popup, select the above options as per your machine and click on the **OK** button.

5. In the WAR directory selected you will now get your **War File** and the dependent file generated with the name of the WAR file mentioned.

6. Once you have the generated the WAR file you may now deploy it to a Tomcat instance.

With this we have come to the end of this chapter.

Summary

In this chapter we have learnt to create mock services and deploy them. We have also learnt to implement a different dispatch type of the service as per our business needs.

The next chapter explains the best practice in SoapUI test automation.

10
Best Practices in SOA Test Automation

In this chapter we will learn the following topics:

- Best practices in SOA testing and test automation
- Why do we need best practices?
- How would the best practices help?

Why do we need best practices?

Best practices are essential for the successful implementation of any automation testing project. Best practices help us to avoid hurdles and help us achieve the desired results in Test Automation with the successful implementation of the framework with minimum maintenance and maximum reusable script.

Best practices are the guidelines following which we face less challenges and gain maximum efficiency.

Like any other test automation, SOA testing also has its best practices as experts have learnt in their career while implementing SOA test automation frameworks.

Let's go through the best practices for SOA test automation

- Choose the right tool
- Get involved early in the development and design phase
- Get the right resources
- Plan candidate for virtualization or service mocking
- Process

- Define candidate for automation
- Dedicated and locked test environment
- Encapsulated framework
- Dynamic assertions
- Three levels in SOA testing
- Perform non-functional tests
- Correct onshore nearshore and offshore ratio
- Utilizing unit test with test automation
- Build good manual test cases
- Is the project mature enough for test automation?

So let's discuss all of these, one-by-one and in detail.

Choose the right tool

Choosing the right tool is really important and the following factors should be considered while choosing an SOA test automation tool:

- **Budget**: budget should be considered an important factor. We should choose the right tools to suit our budget as we might need to buy licenses for each tester if the client doesn't already have the licenses.

- **Protocols support**: We need to identify the protocol supported, as the tool might not support the protocol used in the current project. For example, TCP /IP is not supported by SoapUI but it is supported by IBM RIT [Rational Integration Tester].

- **Message format support**: We need to identify the message supported, as the tool might not support the protocol used in the current project, for example, SWIFT or ISO format messages are not supported by SoapUI, but they are supported by IBM RIT.

- **Training needs**: We need to verify the training needs for the particular tool we are using and also the training cost which takes another toll on the project

- **Tool support**: The tool support should be available and reachable.

- **User reviews**: To verify the right choice it is recommended that we verify the user reviews of the tools on sites like LinkedIn.

- **Virtualization/mock service support**: We need to verify if the tool supports virtualization/Mock Service and also the protocols supported by it.

- **Support for non-functional testing**: Support for non-functional testing is essential and tools should be validated for the support of performance and security testing.

- **Support for UI interactions**: In end-to-end testing we might need to interact with the UI as well, so we might need a tool which may invoke a UI when needed as well; consideration should be given to this point as well. For example, LISA which is also capable of invoking the UI.

Get involved early in the lifecycle

SOA manual and test automation both require early involvement of the test team as SOA testers should not just be technologically skilled, but should also know the business as this will help in creation of better test automation suites.

To best suit the needs of the early involvement of the test team we should use the following V Model:

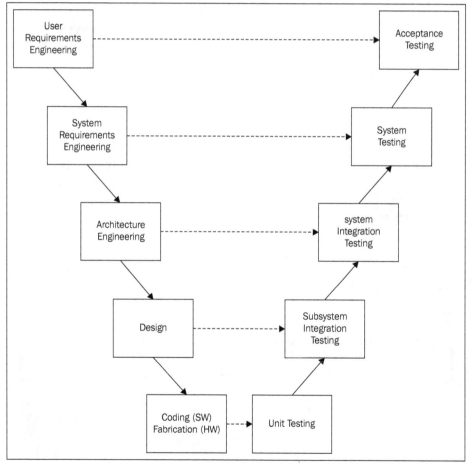

V Model

It is recommended that the V model is implemented in any SOA testing and test automation Project because of the following reason:

- It supports a top down as well as bottom up approach for testing and test automation

- The test levels define each testing in detail and with specifications

- This model facilitates testing at every stage and hence throughout the lifecycle

The preceding points reflect that the V model provides more clarity of the business to the testers as they are involved early. This pays in return with great test cases and great test automation.

Virtualization/mock services support

In any application we have third-party systems, which have their services that need to be tested. At the time of unit testing and integration testing we might not get the real system available to us so we cannot really test the integration between systems hence cannot execute any test.

So what do we do?

We virtualize/mock service the systems which are not available to us.

We should consider the following factors while evaluating a tool for virtualization:

- Protocols supported
- Message formats supported
- Virtualization server cost

The preceding factors, once evaluated, will help you choose a tool from a test virtualization perspective.

 We usually automate third-party services which are not accessible to us for testing ,and hence we should consider the candidate for virtualization/mock service before evaluating the tool for virtualization support.

Get the right resources

It is very important to consider this as we should have the sufficient amount of expertise in the tool we plan to select these for a project. We should evaluate this point based on the following constraint:

- Number of expert resources
- Training required
- Learning curve
- Ease of use
- Any previous experiences in the organization.

The preceding factors would help everyone evaluating the tool for their project.

The testing process in SOA testing should be well defined. Following are some of the factors to validate:

- Define the test-coverage metrics
- End-to-end traceability metrics
- Execution process and tracking
- No ad-hoc testing
- Define the tests
- Define test entry and exit criteria at each stage

Candidate for test automation

It is not possible to automate all the test cases, so it is important to identify the correct candidates for test automation.

The advantage of test automation is that test is repeatable whereas a test whose frequency of execution is less can be taken care by manual testing.

A correct test case candidate for test automation should satisfy the following criteria:

- Repetitive tests and regression tests
- Tests which are complex and may cause human error
- Tests that require multiple data sets
- Critical functionality tests which are used in BAU flows
- Tests that take time to execute
- Tests that are required to be tested on multiple environment with different configurations

Dedicated and locked test environment

It is very important to have a dedicated and a locked test environment for SOA testing and test automation. Usually, it is really important to have a separate environment instead of using the developer's environment. The use of a dedicated test environment provides stability in test results and makes issues traceable.

And adding access controls in the test environment will make sure that the build is not played with by any of the dev or test guys as the access would remain only with the key people.

This approach will really help in the following ways:

- Stable test results
- Good process
- Traceability is easy
- Easy to find defect and replicate them
- Regression testing is easy
- Quality of the test process is improved
- Test works independent of the developer
- No sudden changes are made by developers, testers have control of the environment

Encapsulated test automation framework

The design of any **test automation framework (TAF)** is its most important feature. If the design is good, the framework will be scalable, reliable and efficient with very less maintenance efforts

Considering the way the testing arena has changed over the past decade it is recommended to use encapsulation for your test automation framework.

Encapsulation is the mechanism of wrapping the data (variables) and code acting on the data (methods) together as a single unit.

So we should remember the above statement while we implement encapsulation in our TAF.

 We need to bind data and logic together and teach the test to pick the relevant data from the data sources that will provide intelligence to the framework.

Benefits from TAF encapsulation

Let's see now what we gain from encapsulating our TAF. Following are some of the benefits:

- Run on multiple platforms just by having a parameterized value, which is maintained in an external data source
- Well-defined folder structure
- Better test execution as the test can be taught to run on any platform and use whatever data we choose
- Support for runtime decisions

Dynamic assertions or validations

Let's now have a look at the assertions to be used in the TAF that makes the TAF detect defects.

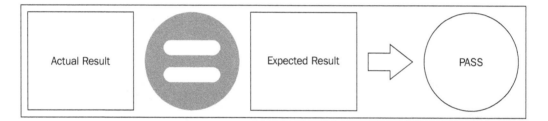

It is very important for any framework to have dynamic assertions rather than having static assertions. In dynamic assertions we validate the data at runtime, based on the input, and fetch the expected results from the desired data source, whereas in static assertion, expected results are static and independent of the data sent in the request.

Let's take a look at a dynamic assertions implementation.

Let's suppose we have a test request and here is the structure of the automated test case:

- Test data import of Groovy script
- Set environment of Groovy script
- Expected results retrieval and storage of Groovy script
- Test request with XPath assertions
- Result logging for reporting purposes

Now here in the above example let's look at a few things:

We import the input test data for the request based on which results would be fetched.

For example, let's suppose the request is a get employee data request and takes Emp ID as its input, which is supplied to it by the test data import step. Now, whenever the Emp ID changes expected results will also change, making any static assertion fail even if they pass.

So to solve this issue we have dynamic assertions.

Lets see how this can be achieved !!

We will now break the task of creating dynamic assertions into three steps.

Step 1: Import Excel data using the following script:

```
import com.eviware.soapui.model.*

import com.eviware.soapui.model.testsuite.Assertable

import com.eviware.soapui.support.XmlHolder

import java.io.File;

import java.util.*;

import jxl.write.*

import jxl.*

def regLogger =
    org.apache.log4j.Logger.getLogger("RegressionTestLoger");

def groovyUtils = new com.eviware.soapui.support.GroovyUtils(
    context )

def properties = new java.util.Properties();/

def s2
Workbook workbook = Workbook.getWorkbook(new File
    ("D:\\import input data.xls"))
```

```
for (count in 2.. 11)
{
  Sheet sheet = workbook.getSheet(1)
  Cell a1 = sheet.getCell(0,count) // getCell(row,column) - place
    some values in myfile.xlsCell b2 =
    sheet.getCell(s3.toInteger(),count) // then those values will
    be acessed using a1, b2 , c3 Cell.
  String s1 = a1.getContents();
  s2 = b2.getContents();
  testRunner.testCase.setPropertyValue(s1,s2);
}

workbook.close()
```

Step 2: Now, when the input data is imported and saved, you can utilize the data and fetch the expected results from the database using the following script:

```
import groovy.sql.Sql;
def regLogger =
  org.apache.log4j.Logger.getLogger("RegressionTestLoger");
def GUID;
def delayStep =
  testRunner.testCase.testSuite.getPropertyValue("delayStep")
def tryCount =
  testRunner.testCase.testSuite.getPropertyValue("delayRetries")
def account = testRunner.testCase.getPropertyValue("EMPID")

int x = 1
int y = 0

while ( x <= Integer.parseInt(tryCount) & y != 1  & y != 2 )
{
    println "Delaying " +  Integer.parseInt(delayStep)* 0.001 + "
seconds."
    Thread.sleep(Integer.parseInt(delayStep))
    def sql =
    groovy.sql.Sql.newInstance
    ("jdbc:oracle:thin:@10.253.10X.20X:1521:XXQA4","XCWDEV4SL",
    "XCWDEV4SL", "oracle.jdbc.driver.OracleDriver")
```

```
row = sql.firstRow ("select  from com_header where EMPID= "  +
EMPID+  "order by cwordercreationdate desc")

testRunner.testCase.setPropertyValue("EMPName",
  GUID.toString ());
testRunner.testCase.setPropertyValue("emp_age",
  age.toString ());
```

Step 3: Now the same can be referred in XPath assertions and then your assertions are dynamic.

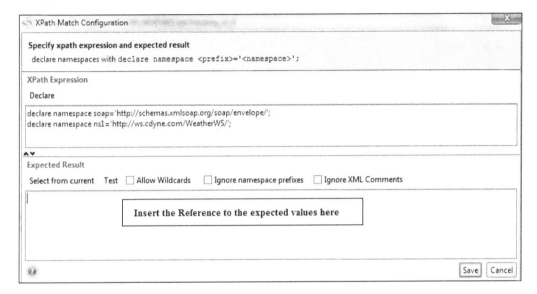

In the **Expected Results** section, you can create a value in the test property at test case level and reference it here. For example, if the property is created at the test case level and the name is Expected V1 then the expression to be put in the expected results would be ${#TestCase#ExpectedV1}. You can also put a static value in the **Expected Result** section.

I am sure we now have a better idea of why dynamic assertions are really good and lie in the best practices list. There are three levels in SOA testing:

To achieve the desired result in SOA testing and test automation we should have three testing phases in SOA testing:

- Unit or component level: testing the components independently
- Integration level: testing the integration between components
- End-to-end testing/system level: testing the implementation as a whole

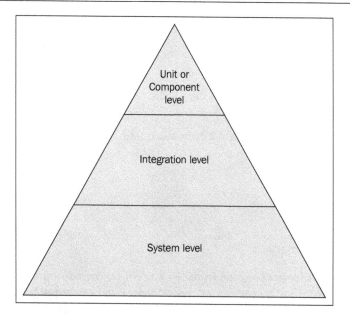

When we define SOA testing in three phases we gain the following benefits:

- **Early identification of defects**: Unit level testing catches the defect early
- **Less defect leakage**: Three levels of SOA testing makes sure that no, or very few, defects are leaked
- **Better process**: The process is better since we have a three-level validation for SOA testing

It can also be said that following the three-level approaches will provide a quality application with better and reusable SOA components.

Performing non-functional tests

Like any other components in a composite application, API and web services can be tested not just from a functionality point of view, but also from a non-functional testing view.

- Security testing - verify the API from a security point of view.

  Test the API for the following tests

  - SQL injection
  - XPATH injection
  - Malformed XML

- ° Boundary scan
- ° Malicious attachment
- ° CSS attack

- Performance, load and stress verify the behavior of single or multiple sets of API under various loads.

  Test the performance of the application using the following performance testing techniques:

  - ° LOAD
  - ° SOAK
  - ° Endurance
  - ° Benchmark

- Interoperability and connectivity – can API be consumed in the agreed manner and does it connect to other components as expected?

APIs are reusable components, and you need to be sure when you are using them, so it's best to have them checked for security and performance earlier than regretting things later. This is because certain API and services exchange highly confidential data which, if exposed, can cause severe loss to a business.

Correct onshore, nearshore and offshore ratios

Let's have a look at the right way of defining project working models:

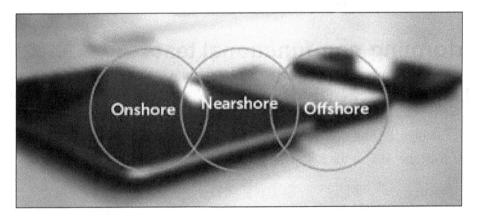

A correct onshore and offshore model is really important in an SOA testing engagement because of the following reasons:

- SOA testers needs to know the business
- SOA testers needs to understand the technology, protocols and so on
- SOA testers are the ones who need access to third-party systems
- SOA testers face environment challenges
- At the time of virtualization we need access to the real system.
- SOA testers start early in the **SDLC** (short for **Software Development Life Cycle**) traditionally following a V model approach

So to sum up, a complete offshore model would not work for an SOA testing engagement, however, a mix ratio of 70 offshore:30 onshore would be ok for an SOA testing engagement.

Or we can look towards an onshore model or a near shore model..

But considering the complexity of the work, experience and expertise would always suggest having people from the team to be onshore.

Utilizing a unit test with test automation

Well let's consider automating our entire component test and placing it as a barrier for build quality acceptance.

Wouldn't this help save manual intervention and make sure only quality and stable build reaches the testers?

This approach will not just help the testers but will also cut costs and effort on the testing front, and would be really helpful in implementing a strong and stable environment which promotes the quality of deliverables from the development end

Here's how to do it:

We have already seen in previous chapters how to integrate Jenkins with SoapUI, so let's revise the steps:

1. Create a unit test in SoapUI
2. Create a batch file or an Ant script to run the tests.
3. Integrate with Jenkins:

The following screenshot will freshen things up on how to achieve this:

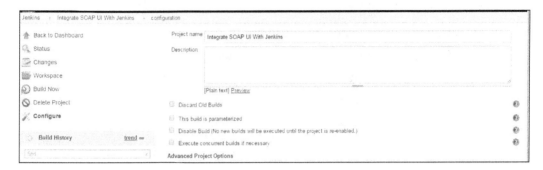

A sample Ant file to run the cases:

```
<arg line= "-j -f 'C:/Users/pnandan/Desktop/Analysis/NewFolder'
  'C:/Users/pnandan/Desktop/Test/Pranai/Production.xml'"/>
  </exec>
  </target>
    <target name = "testreport" depends ="soapui">
    <junitreport todir="C:/Users/pnandan/Desktop/Analysis/NewFolder">
    <fileset dir="C:/Users/pnandan/Desktop/Analysis/NewFolder">
    <include name="TEST-TestSuite_1.xml"/>
  </fileset>
  <report todir="C:/Users/pnandan/Desktop/Analysis/NewFolder/HTML"
  styledir="C:/Testing/apache-ant-1.9.6/etc"
  format="frames">
  </report>
  </junitreport>
  </target>
</project>
```

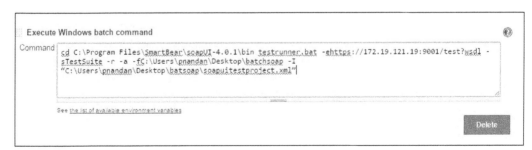

Building good manual test cases

Building good test cases will result in better automation test cases since they will have all the test validations and scenarios covered.

This will not just help the automation testers but also make sure that the automation testing suite adheres to the business requirements and we will have a better suite with most of the requirements being covered.

This will also provide an end-to-end traceability between requirement, manual test cases and automation tests.

With this last topic we come to the end of this chapter and following is the summary of the same.

Summary

In this chapter we have learnt the following:

- Best practices in SOA testing and test automation
- Why do we need best practices
- How would the best practices help

Index

M

manual test cases
building 213
matrix
URL 141
mock services
creating, in SoapUI 180-188
deploying, to external server 196, 197
monitoring tools
JConsole 52
JProfiler 52
multilayer test automation
Selenium used 133, 134
SoapUI used 133, 134

N

non-functional tests
performing 209

P

performance counters, Perfmon
database analysis 69
performance limitations 69
server analysis 68
performance limitations
buffer overflow 69
configuration parameters tuning 69
memory leakage 69
performance testing
analysis phase 52
assertions 63-66
benchmark testing 54
component level 49, 50
delivery phase 53
early visibility testing 54
load testing 55
planning 52
quality gates 56
scenario level 50
SoapUI used 58
stress testing 55
system level 50, 51

test execution phase 55
types 54
workload model 54
performance testing tools
Apache JMeter 51
cURL 52
LoadUI 51
SoapUI 51
post execution steps, Jenkins 162
pre-requisites 70-74
property transfer
configuring 27-29

Q

quality gates
dependency 58
test data 57
test environments 56, 57
Quick Test Professional (QTP) 134

R

random dispatch methods
about 190
configuration 190
Ranorex 135
**requisites, test automation framework
design hybrid**
about 127
reporting 129
test case creation in SoapUI 127, 128
test cases in Excel sheet 127, 128
test data 128, 129
unique data 130, 131
validations 129

S

scripting types
linear scripting 96
modular scripting 96
security testing
attack types 75
examples, in web services 81-83

www.ingramcontent.com/pod-product-compliance
Lightning Source LLC
Chambersburg PA
CBHW060546060326
40690CB00017B/3622